The Fine Art of
WALL DESIGN

by
Suzanne Gallagher

the

ACKNOWLEDGEMENTS

Who would ever have thought that *I*, of all people, would write a book? Never in my wildest dreams, and I love to dream, would I have envisioned accomplishing this feat. As a student my professors would not have encouraged me to pursue this kind of endeavor because my strength certainly was not in the journalistic realm.

Only with the help and collaborative effort and support of Jack, my husband of 35 years, patient friends too numerous to list, clients and creative business associates including my copyright attorney, Patchen Haggerty, graphic designer, Meg Larson, business consultant, volunteer editors, photographer, and other professional interior designers, could I have ever pulled it off! The life lessons and experience along the way is as valuable as the end result.

Kudos to Steve Dodd, President of Northwest Framing, who gave me and my Designers Art Unlimited Associates a resource and opportunity to offer beautiful art and custom framing to our interior design customers. Without this quality resource I would not have developed the expertise and inspiration for "The Fine Art of Wall Design."

Completion of this book is a testimony to the fact that with vision, determination and a little naïveté, anything is possible. ALTA Press is in honor of my dear mother Alta Jackson Matthaeus who at this writing has lived 90 years. She attended grades 1-8 in a one room schoolhouse on ranch property donated to the rural Weiser, Idaho community by her father. Her life example and wise counsel has continually been a blessing in my life.

I would be irreverent not to give ultimate credit to the divine intervention of our Almighty God who continually provides amazing miracles!

Suzanne
Gallagher

The
WALL DESIGN *Diva*

Thank You...

for sharing my passion for The Fine Art of Wall Design! It may interest you to know how I came to the conclusion that "wall design" had a place of its own in the interior design world.

I really didn't intend to become the "Wall Design Diva" when I graduated from the University of Washington, Seattle, with a BS in Textiles, Clothing and Art. In fact, after leaving Seattle for the real world I began my career working for a textile print company in Honolulu, assisting the stylist with her job of selecting and adapting gorgeous designs for fabric to be used by bikini and aloha shirt manufacturers!

After my engagement to Jack, my wonderful husband of over 35 years, I returned to the mainland to plan THE wedding. Shortly after, we moved to San Francisco where I worked as a management trainee in retail, then a merchandiser for a sportswear manufacturer and eventually landed a position with I.Magnin and Co. as their Fashion Coordinator. You know, that's the lucky person who produces those glamorous shows with all the New York designers! Oh yes, I worked with Bill Blass, Halston, Tassell of the House of Norell, Calvin Klein when he was showing his first collections, the Nipons, etc. From there our family moved to New York where I worked for Saks Fifth Avenue producing their shows. What a fun time! Our first child was born in San Francisco, just 6 weeks before moving to the Plaza in New York where Jack worked as a manager for Westin Hotels.

The bustle of New York and, let's face it, the cost of living and our yearning to return to the west coast and family led us back to Portland, Oregon. There I did some free lance work and pretty much became a full-time mom after another son and daughter filled our nest.

It was when we moved into our "new home," the second house, that my interest in framed art really began to blossom. This home was more than twice the size of the first one, and our old furniture looked wrong and bad. We had almost no art pieces, save for the few that I painted myself while in New York. Art and home furnishings had just not been a priority while the kids were young.

Even though we weren't able to purchase furnishings right away, I just had to have something on the walls in key locations to serve as focal points in each room. I knew that this house would not feel like a home until there was something that reflected "us" in our interior spaces. I discovered a great national art framing resource, who supplied interior designers with frame samples, mat corners and training in framing design, for a relatively small investment. They had a program allowing professionals the opportunity to provide in-home service, offer retail pricing, and make a good profit! I went for it as I wanted an art and framing resource as well as income for the other furnishings our home was lacking! My sales were tops in the nation, and I brought other designers into the business as well, allowing me to enjoy additional income. What fun! Alas, after six years of success, my supplier went out of business. I turned my sales force, client base, experience and knowledge into an even more successful business, this time with Northwest Framing, a West Coast commercial art framing company.

Today, I continue to serve clients with their art and interior needs. I have found that it is the art décor that makes the space personal, reflecting the passions of the home and office owners. Art is most often the focal point of every room. It is the glue that brings the interior furnishings together!

Suzanne

CONTENTS

3 IT'S ALL IN THE DESIGN!

4 EVERYTHING IN ITS PLACE!

5 APPENDIX

FIVE MOST COMMON WALL DESIGN MISTAKES:

1. **People choose the wrong art image for their interior décor.**
   Often times the art is the wrong size or colors are not in keeping with their room colors.
   In addition, the style may be wrong for the style of the room.

2. **The framing design choice is wrong for the art piece.**
   People often take their art to a framer who knows very little about classic framing design. The art may be technically framed incorrectly, utilizing the wrong materials and design proportion.

3. **The framing design is wrong for the space.**
   It is possible and desirable to design the framing for the art <u>and</u> the décor.
   For example, a small image may be matted to a size that will accommodate a rather large space if designed correctly.

4. **Placement on the wall is also a big problem, not only for the home but also commercial spaces.** Usually the art is hung too high. Pairs and groupings are seldom hung appropriately.

5. **Mirrors are often hung is the wrong spaces, where they reflect nothing of interest.**
   When appropriately placed a mirror can reflect something beautiful and expand the interior space.

Solutions to follow!

Do you want to achieve a look in your home décor that is unique and represents *your* personality, *your* unique style? The choices that are necessary to complete the design of an interior space seem endless – from the flooring, wall finishes and colors to window coverings, upholstery and wood furnishings. Images in magazines beckon us to try this design "look" or that, never quite representing *your* individual uniqueness.

I have been helping clients in their homes and businesses with their art selection, framing design, and placement for over twelve years. My discovery: wall décor is as important, if not more important, as all the other elements of the space combined. It reflects the personality of the owner and defines the mood in the room. Art is one of the most exciting and emotionally gratifying purchases you will make. However, the "If you love it, buy it!" principle is really not applicable unless you have mastered the basics of the Fine Art of Wall Design. You may take your art purchase home only to discover that the frame style is wrong, or the colors in the art do not work or, even more frustrating, *The size is not right!*

You are now about to discover the thrill of knowing how to select, design and place art correctly and creatively. Welcome to the Fine Art of Wall Design!

Start with art!

WHAT IS THE FINE ART OF WALL DESIGN?

When I began teaching this concept in a seminar setting, I realized that there was no *official* definition for the term, "Fine Art of Wall Design." I was getting the idea across to my attendees in great style. The only thing missing was a succinct definition of the concept.

Since it is my very own term, I can come up with my own definition, right? With all due respect to Webster, et al., here goes: The Fine Art of Wall Design is the arrangement of art, objects and mirrors on interior wall space. Seems simple enough.

But, The Fine Art of Wall Design is definitely more than that! It implies a higher level of design, incorporating all the elements necessary to achieve excellence in interior space. Therefore, let us go one step further. **The Fine Art of Wall Design® is achieved when the image, color, style, framing design, and placement combine with the interior space to create a dynamic look and feel.**

And you know you have achieved the Fine Art of Wall Design® when you can express "Va Va Voom", "Ooh La La", "WOW!", "Ah Hah" and "That's it!"

©LOMA SMITH PHOTOGRAPHY

15

TEST YOUR WALL DESIGN I.Q.

1 What is the best reason to display art in your home?
- **a.** To cover holes left by previous owner.
- **b.** To fill blank spaces on your walls.
- **c.** To create interest and personality in your personal living space.

2 The average home has wall space for approximately
- **a.** 10 – 20 pieces of art
- **b.** 20 – 30 pieces of art
- **c.** 30 – 50 pieces of art

3 The most costly part of interior design is the wall art.
- **a.** True
- **b.** False

4 Custom framed art is really not a good investment.
- **a.** True
- **b.** False

5 "Wall Design" is:
- **a.** The application of color to walls.
- **b.** A term applied to the application of texture to walls.
- **c.** The selection and arrangement of art, objects, and mirrors on interior wall space.

6 One should consider art selection when first beginning a design project because it is easier to find other décor to go with art choices than visa versa.
- **a.** True
- **b.** False

7 Mirrors are not considered an integral part of wall design.
- **a.** True
- **b.** False

8 At least how many times should an accent color be placed in a room?
   a. 2
   b. 3
   c. 5

9 One easy way to create a new and fresh look in a room is through the placement of art.
   a. True
   b. False

10 The style known as "country" has gone *out* in recent years.
   a. True
   b. False

11 When selecting art, the greatest consideration should be given to the style of the room.
   a. True
   b. False

12 What is the best way to add accent colors in a room?
   a. Add pillows in different colors.
   b. Place one or more pieces of art in a prominent place.
   c. All of the above.

Number Correct _____

I.Q. RATING
10-12 . . .Wow, I'm impressed!
7-9 . . .You're doing great!
4-6 . . .You have potential!
3-5 . . .I have a mission!
0-2 . . .Glad you are here!

WHY DO YOU DISPLAY ART?

Why do we see a space and yearn for an image to be placed right <u>there</u>? What does it do for the room? What does it do for you?

Art creates the center of interest and often an element of surprise in any space. We need something pleasant to rest our eyes on. It sets the tone and mood in the space. Art adds color and interest, and it can also pull the colors and themes in your décor together.

Color is a strong element that influences our attraction to art. Pay attention to your color preferences in art. I find that I wear the colors I prefer in my home decor. We are usually drawn to scenes that have a common dominant color again and again. Art imagery is a wonderful source for color in interior décor.

Basic **emotional attraction** cannot be overlooked amongst the reasons to display art. We love an image because of how it makes us feel! Do you get excited about lots of change and variety in your life? Are you about fun or do you yearn for tranquility and simplicity? All of these emotional elements are found in the artist's interpretation of color and form. Are you that person who collects stuff and loves to display things relating to your passions. Those collectibles can become art if framed properly!

Art will set a **tone, mood or ambiance** in your interior spaces. It can carry out a theme that you are working to achieve, and repeat design elements in the space. For example, if you desire to create a tropical mood, display images of exotic beaches and palm trees!

More importantly, art is an **expression of your unique style** and personality. Often times we see an image and are drawn to it not knowing why. Somehow it just captures the vision you had in mind. It just calls your name!

I DISPLAY ART FOR THE FOLLOWING REASONS:

1. _____
_____
_____
_____
_____

2. _____
_____
_____
_____

3. _____
_____
_____
_____

4. _____
_____
_____
_____

SUZANNE GALLAGHER, WALL DESIGN DIVA

Can you imagine this room without art? The style of the Leroy Neiman piece gives this space such character. It sets the tone. Art warms up this space.

A room feels incomplete even though it is full of furniture. You may have selected all the chairs, tables, sofas and armoire for your room only to realize that it just is not enough. The space feels bare and uninteresting. You need art!

LAURIE BANNON, DESIGNER

©RUSS WIDSTRAND

Art can be the least costly part of interior decorating. Just add up the cost of your sofa, chairs, tables, window coverings, area rugs, carpet, wall paper and other furnishings! If you have shopped for upholstery, wood pieces, window coverings, and floor coverings lately, you will agree that one or more pieces of framed art is a small purchase in comparison. Granted, there are some art originals that go for thousands, but the average homeowner will not be in the market for something in that price range. Think of the art as furniture or "jewelry" on your walls.

Problem: We often spend the entire decorating budget on furniture, allowing nothing for art and accessories.

Solution: It is a good rule to allow at least 30% of your decorating budget for art and accessories when embarking on a design project.

There is no accent color here except for the beautiful painting placed over the buffet. It introduces opportunity to repeat those colors in other areas of the room!

GREEN WITH ENVY INTERIORS

There is more square footage of wall space than anything else in our homes. If you took the walls and laid them down on the ground, there would be about twice the space as you have on the floor! Of course we have windows and doors or doorways so that takes care of some space, but for the most part we have a lot of opportunity to hang art.

©BRUCE FORSTER

RENAISSANCE HOMES

CAN YOU OWN TOO MUCH ART?

The average home has space for approximately 30 to 50 pieces of art. As home construction has evolved in recent years, we have seen the ceilings become higher and space more generous. Stairways are voluminous. Everything is just on a larger scale. There is more wall space!

©RUSS WIDSTRAND

SUZANNE GALLAGHER, WALL DESIGN DIVA

Count the items of wall décor in this kitchen space. There are 7. Multiply that by just five spaces and you are up to 35!

You don't believe it? Take a tour of your home and count the wall décor pieces, including mirrors, then add those bare spots that need something. Between family pictures and decorative art and wall objects, the numbers are surprising. My experience in furnishing show homes has substantiated this phenomenon. If you don't have nearly 30, you need more!

MY ART/MIRROR INVENTORY:

Entry/Hall_____   Staircase_____

Study_____   Downstairs Bath_____

Living Room_____   Dining Room_____

Family Room_____   Kitchen_____

Bedroom 1_____   Bedroom 2_____

Bedroom 3_____   Bedroom 4_____

Master Bedroom_____   Master Bath_____

Other_____

Total_____

When viewing a photograph of an interior space such as this, I often wonder what inspired the designer. Was it the art? In this example, I have to think that the abstract image in this dining room was the inspiration for the design!

KIMBERLEE JAYNES INTERIOR DESIGNS, INC.

WHAT IS YOUR STYLE?

Can you answer this question? Most of us can't because styles today are loosely defined and easily interchangeable. A room should be defined not by style, but by how it makes you feel. When first talking with prospective clients on the phone I ask this question, only to discover when stepping into their home that they really did not know the name or description of the style they have or actually prefer. Let's take an opportunity to identify some of the most common styles and determine yours in the process, shall we?

Traditional – Luxurious, Proper, Elegant

Tried and true, the classic styling of the "traditional" interior is timeless, at least for our duration on this earth! We can easily incorporate furniture and accessory pieces into this décor from our ancestors who invested in these timeless looks! Recently the term "Old World" is used in reference to define a feel of European design dating to times reminiscent of the Renaissance period and beyond. It gives us a sense of history and permanence. In this case "old" is very good. This style tends to be more formal than not and is usually seen in living and dining and master bedroom spaces. Easterners are especially fond of the traditional as its historical roots are there. It is fun to mix styles and periods within this genre.

SUE RAYMOND, DESIGNER

Casual Traditional – Comfortable, Practical, Timeless

The contemporary big furniture and furnishings retailers are definitely setting the stage for a new style. I call it "Casual Traditional." The look is comfortable, simple and incorporates elements from the wonderful timeless looks of the more formal classic traditional. Most people can relate to this look. It's not too masculine or feminine, just good design. The pieces can be easily incorporated with inherited pieces or items collected by any homeowner.

Is this **your** style? There is something very practical about it. The permanence and timelessness of traditional furniture lines is stable. It transitions and mixes with modern as well as antique looks. It works for almost everyone.

SUE RAYMOND, DESIGNER

©RUSS WIDSTRAND

Down to Earth – Sophisticated, Upscale Comfort

The current trend in building materials toward everything natural in design is timeless and permanent. The application of beautiful stone, slate, and exotic hardwoods exudes a richness that surpasses most things man made. Colors are easy to live with. The look adapts to all styles of furnishings. The wing back chairs in this dining room are a lovely reminder of classic style.

©BRUCE FORSTER

RENAISSANCE HOMES

Country – English, American, Swedish

Remember when this term was first introduced to the buying public? It seemed that the look just took over! Everything was pink and blue, plaid, and accessories were heavy with handmade items including baskets, straw floral arrangements, hand painting, and the "Goose Girl" image in every home! Now the reference to country is broad, encompassing the "country" look of many countries. For example, we see Swedish, French, English and New England Country. All styles are unique and wonderful in their own right. The look is casual, and I consider it to be quite timeless in its traditionalism.

KP DESIGN GROUP, INC.

Modern – Edgy, Upbeat

Sometimes we hear this style referred to as "contemporary." Well, if you think about it, "contemporary" is literally "today." Depending on when today is, that could be most anything! So, the look should really be called "modern." You've seen it. The wonderful clean lines that represent this look along with bold blocks of color make it very up to date at any time.

Craftsman, Lodge – Rustic, Rugged

The "craftsman" feel has made a huge comeback in the Northwest. It represents such artisans as Stickley and architectural elements reminiscent of Frank Lloyd Wright. In addition we see a leaning in this category toward the "lodge" feel. It is appealing to the outdoors lovers. We love to live in spaces that reflect our hobbies and interests. I see this style often when the owners are into hunting, fishing, winter sports, and camping. It is truly comfortable and incorporates interesting accessories and furniture.

GREEN WITH ENVY INTERIORS

LAURIE BANNON, DESIGNER

Classic Modern –
Minimal, Simple, Carefree

The emphasis is on simplicity, neutral colors and very minimal accessory application. It is a sophisticated look. Another term I associate with this look is "metropolitan." It reminds me of the time represented by such novels as The Fountainhead and Atlas Shrugged. People who lean toward this style are usually professionals with busy lives and are seeking solace and a lack of clutter and distraction in their homes.

Eclectic - Interesting, Stimulating, Creative

Most of us fall into this interior style category. For reasons that may be purely practical, we enjoy the acceptance of combining two or more style elements in our interior spaces. What could be more interesting than the mix of "modern," Asian and "traditional?" This room utilizes the wonderful permanence of neutral colors, traditional sofas, Asian tables, and a modern abstract painting for pizzaz!

KP DESIGN GROUP, INC.

WHAT IS YOUR COLOR SCHEME?

Color! You must decide! It is so important to the feel of your room. It is the ribbon that ties the spaces together. Don't be afraid to use it. Sometimes the toughest part is just deciding on a scheme. There are so many options!

Elegant Color

KP DESIGN GROUP, INC.

KIMBERLEE JAYNES INTERIOR DESIGNS, INC.

M FRANCES INTERIORS ©RUSS WIDSTRAND

RENE KATHLEEN INTERIORS

40

KP DESIGN GROUP, INC.

TITUS BY DESIGN

Have I mentioned that there are no hard and fast rules when it comes to design? However, there are some guidelines that are helpful to keep in mind. Those relating to color are no exception. I suggest that you divide the amounts of color you are using in your spaces into three categories:

Dominant
❑ 40% - 50%
❑ Usually wall or floor color

Secondary
❑ 30% - 40%
❑ Furniture, upholstery color

Accent
❑ 20% - 25%
❑ Art, accessories

MY COLORS ARE:

Living Room

Dominant _____

Secondary _____

Accents _____

_____

_____

Dining Room

Dominant _____

Secondary _____

Accents _____

_____

_____

Keep your scheme simple and consistent. Create different moods from room to room by interchanging the dominant color with the secondary color. Also, use different intensities or shades of color from room to room. This way you can interchange furnishings as you proceed with your decorating. If color flows, the furnishings can flow, too, as you add new items to your décor. I often move something from one room to another as the project emerges. If the colors are compatible and set the theme of the overall scheme in your home, then you will have no problem re-locating your art pieces as you add to your home gallery!

Photo on opposite page is the entry of the home and living room shown here. The colors flow beautifully!

M FRANCES INTERIORS ©RUSS WIDSTRAND

YES, START WITH ART!

We have explored the process of determining the **style** and **colors** of our interior spaces; but what do you do when there are no inspirations for color or style? In other words, it is not easy to decide these things when you have no point of reference, nothing to start with. It is hard to know where to start, isn't it? For example, if you have a sofa that you must keep, then you may start with that. At least you have a color and possibly a style.

There is another way of approaching the design process. Begin with your art selection. Choose a piece of art for the focal point of your room. When I meet with a client for the first time, my goal is to learn about their unique style. I cut to the chase quickly so that we can begin making furnishing selections and specifying other design elements. Choice of art is the best clue to style and color preference. We begin by browsing through art catalogs. Try this approach to your design project. You can determine your colors and style easily when you have a piece of art in mind. The discoveries are amazing!

START WITH ART TO DETERMINE YOUR COLOR SCHEME

Pretend you are planning to redo your dining room. This would be a wonderful art image for the space. There are so many rich colors to work with! The TAN shade is excellent for wall color. You could paint the ceiling in CLARET and use the other colors for the chair covers and accessories. Another approach would be to paint the walls red. The blue would be fabulous used in glassware!

What colors could you choose for this room?

Dominant _____

Secondary _____

Accent _____

IRIS NINE PATCH II   CANADIAN ART PRINTS

Don't you just love black and white photography? This kind of image can be very dramatic, if presented well. Take a look at the color swatches here. The citrus lime green is wonderful! Think of another accent that you might put in its place. Depending on the image, black and white art is wonderful in most spaces, but be creative. Let it inspire the room design!

CANADIAN ART PRINTS

SILHOUETTE OAK, WILLIAM GUION

What colors could you choose for this room?

Dominant _____

Secondary _____

Accent _____

48

Blue is coming back! This image is busting with color inspiration that is new. The colors that I have pulled out of this wonderful landscape image by Ken Elliott are a calming pallet of cool natural neutrals. Any combination of two or more shades will create a room to live for!

What colors could you choose for this room?

Dominant _____

Secondary _____

Accent _____

APPROACHING HEAVEN, BROOKS ANDERSON

EDITIONS LIMITED GALLERIES

What colors could you choose for this room?

Dominant _____

Secondary _____

Accent _____

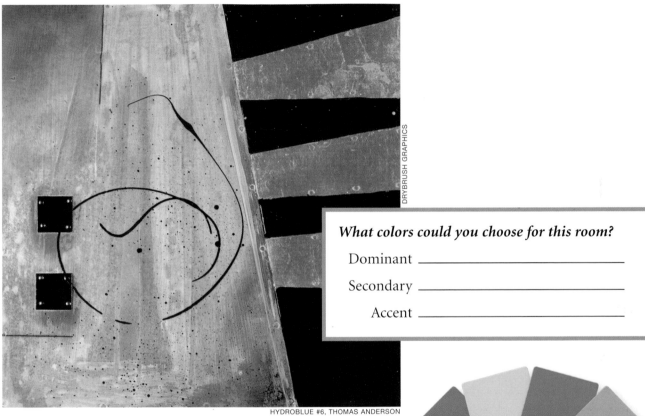

DRYBRUSH GRAPHICS

HYDROBLUE #6, THOMAS ANDERSON

What colors could you choose for this room?

Dominant _____

Secondary _____

Accent _____

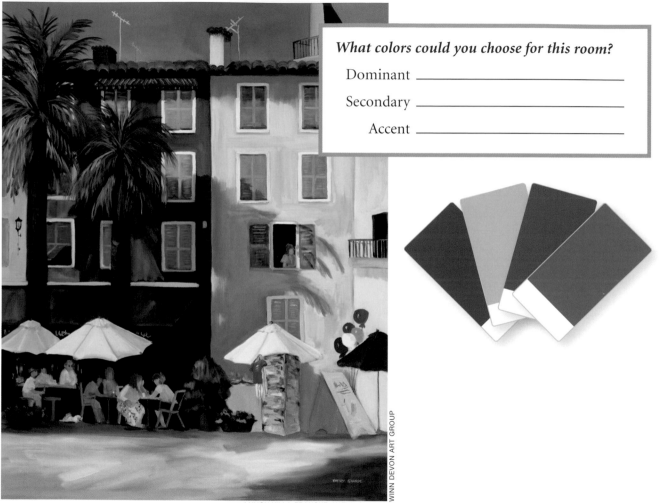

LUNCH VILLA-FRANCHE, KATHY SHARPE

WINN DEVON ART GROUP

What colors could you choose for this room?

Dominant _____

Secondary _____

Accent _____

START WITH ART TO DETERMINE YOUR COLOR SCHEME

SUZANNE GALLAGHER, WALL DESIGN DIVA

START WITH ART TO DETERMINE YOUR STYLE.

Spend some time looking at a variety of different images. It is amazing how you will be attracted to images that are related by color and style. Ask yourself what you like about them. For example, one subject for the artist is "floral still life." There are endless images available in this subject category. Let's take a look at a few and discuss the styles.

I can see a touch of Asian influence in this piece by Terri Burris. It is an abstract but is also clearly a floral still life. It also would lend to the look seen in "classic modern."

BORDEAUX SKY, TERRI BURRIS

WINN DEVON ART GROUP

Another beautiful floral still life image, this piece would enhance any home but the style that comes to my mind is definitely country or casual traditional!

DAISIES AND DELPHINIUMS, VICTOR SANTOS

This image is also a modern floral still life, but it is decidedly different from the one we pictured on page 54 by Terri Burris in color and feeling. The whimsical care free look in "Pink Flowers" is divine. Your space will have a decidedly casual fresh feeling. Does the Modern style - bold colors, clean lines - fit this look?

PINK FLOWERS, CHARLOTTE FOUST

56

CLASSICAL ELEGANCE, JENNIE TOMAO

Are you getting the "picture," no pun intended!
This lovely image features pink flowers also,
but there is no hint of modern style here.
I would say traditional is the style, no contest!
Even the title of the piece screams formal.

I'm wild about this piece by Liz Jardine. It is transitional, in other words it can adapt to almost any style. When placed in a room where the colors compliment, this piece will be a stunner!

POPPY SERENADE, LIZ JARDINE

PINK FLOWERS, CHARLOTTE FOUST

WINN DEVON ART GROUP

PRIMO I, ERIC WAUGH

TOP ART

LUNCH VILLA-FRANCHE, KATHY SHARP

WINN DEVON ART GROUP

Pull your space together with the piece of art you love most. Then add other images incorporating colors and other image subjects for variety and interest!

These pieces nicely compliment one another.
What other wall color could you use in this
room? How about gold?

POPPY SERENADE, LIZ JARDINE

WINN DEVON ART GROUP

FEMME ALLONGEE, DAN BENNION

TOP ART

RED TREES II, SETH WINEGAR

NEW YORK GRAPHIC SOCIETY

SILHOUETTE OAK, WILLIAM GUION

CANADIAN ART PRINTS

BORDEAUX SKY, TERRI BURRIS

WINN DEVON ART GROUP

THE SINGING BUTLER, JACK VETTRIANO

IMAGE CONSCIOUS

Again, different image subjects and styles can work wonderfully together. The link to making it work is color.

When you need design inspiration, START WITH ART!

©RUSS WIDSTRAND

SUZANNE GALLAGHER, WALL DESIGN DIVA

If you are an art collector, furnish your home in neutral colors so that your art can take center stage!
Even though the room color is neutral the colors in the art imagery relate and compliment
each other creating cohesiveness in the space.

The Fine Art of Wall Design® is achieved when the image, color, style, framing design, and placement combine with the interior space to create a dynamic look and feel.

So, how do you know when you have achieved The Fine Art of Wall Design®? When you can express "Va Va Voom", "Ooh La La", "WOW!", "Ah Hah" and "That's it!"

We display art because it expresses our unique style and personality and is truly the glue that pulls a room together. It puts your unique "personal stamp" on your interior spaces!

> Start with art! It is *usually* the focal point of any room and can be the inspiration for the colors and style that you are seeking. The selection of one color out of a fan deck of thousands is far more challenging than choosing an image you love. Find the art first and then bring together colors and furnishings with it in mind!

Next, we will explore the many sources available for art images and some tips for selecting the "right" one – are you ready?

Choosing the "right" image

HOW DO YOU KNOW WHAT IS "RIGHT?"

How do you know what image will be "right" for your interior space? You loved it when you first saw it in the store. It reminded you of the place where you grew up or that fabulous vacation you took two years ago. Maybe the colors were among your favorites. It just seemed to evoke the right mood for your room...

Have you ever shopped for art and carried home a framed piece only to discover that it was the wrong size...shape... or feeling! Something just didn't work.

These are common challenges that consumers have when choosing <u>anything</u> for their home. Some of us will never have the flair that it takes to make great interior design decisions, but **most** can learn simple guidelines, apply basic principles and achieve a magnificent look!

©LOMA SMITH PHOTOGRAPHY

IMAGE COLOR

The color of an image can definitely enhance or detract from the space. Consider repeating the colors in the space when selecting art. Take the opportunity to introduce additional colors in your space that appear in the art, colors that can be incorporated as accents. Art is the perfect inspiration for color!

Design Tip:
Repeat accent color at least three times in your room. Place it at three levels; high, medium and low. Art is the answer for accent color at eye level!

KIMBERLEE JAYNES INTERIOR DESIGNS, INC.

IMAGE STYLE

Another consideration when searching for art is the style of your space. Or better yet, _your_ unique style! There are no rules; however, good design and smooth color transition is the key.

Everyone agrees that variety is the spice of life and interior design is no exception. As you become confident with art selection, you may want to mix different styles of art. Carry out a theme or add an element of surprise!

Reproduction art publishing companies work hard to categorize their images so that the customer can easily find them. Can't you just imagine the creative team of an art publishing company gathered around the conference table deliberating which category to place an image for their new catalog? Subject names are given to sections of their catalogs such as "contemporary," "animals," "abstract," "architecture," "culinary," "classical," "European artists," etc. Some of these descriptions apply to the subject matter and others describe the style of the art.

The designations do not necessarily indicate appropriateness for a particular décor. It is important to remember that the images are placed in these various categories by committee and could quite easily fit into a variety of areas. When searching for an image, keep an open mind and look at everything. Be adventuresome. You will be surprised what you will find in the section called "contemporary" or "abstract" that will work fabulously in a traditional space! It's the color relationship as well as size that contribute most to design compatibility of an image.

Which one of these images would work best in a modern style room? It might be fun to go with the unexpected!

THE STORY BOOK, WILLIAM ADOLPHE BOUGUEREAU

NEW YORK GRAPHIC SOCIETY

WOMAN IN CRIMSON MOSAIC,
CYNTHIA MARKERT

IMAGE CONSCIOUS

MORNING REMEMBRANCE, GHOLAM YUNESSI

WILD APPLE GRAPHICS

FIGURE II, ELENA ILKU

GRAND IMAGE

IMAGE SIZE AND SHAPE

When you have a location in mind, there are guidelines to follow when choosing art. There may be limitations to the size of the image that will fit into the space you are decorating. If the art image is printed on paper, you can design the matting to accommodate a larger space. If the art is canvas, then you are more limited in your options to change the size from small to large.

Is your space one in which the image should be Portrait, taller than wide? Or is it best to have a Landscape shape, wider than tall? Maybe it should be Square? You will learn more about this in the following chapters on framing design and placement. It is a definite consideration when shopping for the best image.

SOURCES FOR ART...
MORE THAN YOU CAN IMAGINE!

My parents' generation had few options for art resources. Original art was essentially the only option available. Now, no matter what your income level, there is something you can afford!

As with all product purchases, it is vital to understand what you are buying! The possibilities are endless. Product knowledge is everything when making buying decisions and art is no exception. In fact, the average consumer has very little understanding of the art reproduction industry. There are many forms of wall art available today from open edition images to original works. When you are unaware of these differences, making an art purchase can be intimidating.

I promise that when you are finished reading this chapter, you will be empowered to discuss the differences with your friends and retailers and confidently make buying decisions when you next shop for art!

OPEN-EDITION REPRODUCTIONS

Open edition reproductions are images that most people can afford. The original images are obtained from artists by publishing companies who then reproduce the images and market to the art industry. The images are photo-mechanically reproduced, utilizing four-color lithography. There are no restrictions as to the number of copies that will be made. This is called an open edition. So, you may see the images used in many ways in the marketplace. Companies who produce framed art for sale in retail stores, internet sources, etc. purchase open edition art.

The original images are varied in style and medium, from oils and acrylics, watercolor, colored pencil to a combination of pastels, metal and collages. They also come in a wide range of sizes from 4" x 4" to 40" x 60". Some of the special features incorporated in the open-edition images are foiling, metallic inks, embossing and varnishes, as well as UV protective coating.

Many of the open-edition catalogs are available for you to peruse at your convenience. If you have not yet explored the amazing images available from these sources, you must make this experience a priority. You can find these images at your local picture framing store or online.

Design Tip:
It is acceptable to "crop" an open-edition reproduction image for framing. I often turn an abstract another direction, or create two images out of one.

On the open-edition market, the imagery styles and sizes are endless! The publishing companies who have sites on the internet do not usually sell direct to the consumer, protecting their relationship with the trade; however, why not become familiar with the wide range of images available? Once you have found that perfect image, it can then be purchased from your local dealer/retailer.

HIGH AND MIGHTY, DON LI-LEGER

CANADIAN ART PRINTS

INTERIOR SETTING I, EVE

CANADIAN ART PRINTS

CLASSIC SCROLL I, PABLO SEGOVIA

TOP ART

LILY MUSCADET, STEVEN MEYERS

POEMS ART, LTD.

MARILYN MANROE, 1952, UNKNOWN

IMAGE CONSCIOUS

AUX COULEURS VIVES I, SHIRLY NOVAK

WILD APPLE GRAPHICS

LA SIGNORA DEL GIARDINO DI TUSCANA, GREG SINGLEY

NEW YORK GRAPHIC SOCIETY

FIELDS OF GOLD, ROBERTO LOMBARDI

EDITIONS LIMITED GALLERIES

JEAN PIERRE, WILL RAFUSE

CANADIAN ART PRINTS

57TH STREET, CAROL JESSEN

EDITIONS LIMITED GALLERIES

GROOVIN', EVE

CANADIAN ART PRINTS

TOP 13

WALL DESIGN DIVA'S
TOP 13 ART PUBLISHERS

Canadian Art Prints	www.canadianartprints.com
Drybrush Graphics	www.drybrushgraphics.com
Editions Limited	www.editionslimited.com
Grand Image	www.grandimage.com
Haddad's Fine Arts, Inc.	www.haddadsfinearts.com
Image Conscious	www.imageconscious.com
New York Graphic Society	www.nygs.com
Old World Prints	www.oldworldprintsltd.com
Poems Art, Ltd.	www.poemsart.com
The Art Group	www.artgroup.com
Top Art	www.topartweb.com
Wild Apple Graphics	www.wildapple.com
Winn Devon Art Group	www.winndevon.com

CANVAS TRANSFER

Canvas transfer is a unique process in which open-edition art can be miraculously transferred to canvas from paper on which it was printed. I will explain this process without revealing the trade "secrets."

We begin with an image printed on paper. This is usually a fine-art reproduction printed on high-quality paper. The most appropriate images are those that were originally painted in oil, acrylic or a mixed media.

Next, the art is sprayed at least two times with a clear medium. When it is thoroughly dry, the art is soaked in a solution of water and emulsion. Then the technician carefully separates the paper from the back of the piece, now suspended in the clear medium, leaving a transparent image. The technician transfers the image onto canvas, making sure that there are no wrinkles or tears in the delicate transfer.

After the canvas dries, the image is appropriately enhanced by an artist, following the original with clear brush strokes. This creates a realistic image resembling the original. If brush strokes are not visible in the original, they are not applied. The canvas transfer technology is another way to bring beautiful art reproductions into the home and office for a reasonable price. Anyone can afford art that appears original!

LAMINATE

An alternative to the canvas transfer is to laminate. It is especially good for areas where there may be excessive moisture, such as a bathroom, spa or cooking space. The print is laminated to pressboard and sealed with a waterproof product. Brush strokes may be added. Both the canvas transfer and the laminate are never recommended for fine art pieces.

TRUE "POSTER" ART

The term "poster" art has commonly been used to refer to all open edition publications, however the strict definition refers to an art medium that was developed from the ancient practice of "posting" messages in public places. Posters were designed to communicate quickly and graphically and were used for advertising or other communication needs. Movies, concerts, plays and other public events all are promoted with posters today.

Famous posters today have become a popular art subject. There is always graphic type on a poster, which is the primary difference between these and other open edition reproductions.

CLIPPER 314, MICHAEL L. KUNGL

HADDAD'S FINE ARTS

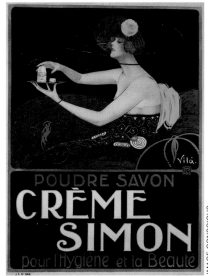

CRÈME SIMON, VILA

IMAGE CONSCIOUS

VINTAGE POSTERS

Vintage posters were printed 50 to 100 years ago and are extremely collectable with a high investment value. These often are large and very graphic, with subject matter ranging from entertainment events to advertisements for products such as tobacco, wine and household items.

HAND COLORED FINE ART PRINTS

Hand colored fine art prints are yet another form of imagery that begs our attention. The creative process begins with a hand-pulled black & white image. Each print is then individually designed and hand colored using the same methods of color application that were used throughout the 19th century before modern, color lithography. Artists meticulously paint each piece using the finest European watercolor paints on heavy, cotton rag archival paper. By combining old world craftsmanship with fresh design innovations, artists create works of stunning depth and vibrancy that are absolutely beautiful and unique.

WHIMSICAL DRAGONFLIES II

OLD WORLD PRINTS

PETITE FINIAL ON BLACK II

OLD WORLD PRINTS

PASSIONATE PEONIES

OLD WORLD PRINTS

LET'S PLAY BILLIARDS II

OLD WORLD PRINTS

CHOCOLATE AND BLUE ROSETTE I

OLD WORLD PRINTS

77

LIMITED-EDITION ART...A STEP UP

Limited edition art can ensure the owner that they will not find their image hanging on the wall in the local discount store or on a plate. If you cannot afford to invest in a well known artist's original, you will want to investigate the world of limited edition art.

In art, a limited edition means that there are a limited number of images in a published edition. Once the pre-determined number of impressions are made, no more impressions are to be taken; assuring that the edition is "limited." The number of impressions in a limited edition is information that should be available to the consumer, especially if the price reflects the scarcity of the piece. Both original graphics and reproductions are offered as "limited editions" from artists and art publishers.

At the bottom of each print in an edition, the artist pencils in his signature and numbers the print. The numbering appears as one number over another; for example, 15/30. This indicates that this was the 15th print to be signed and there are a total of 30 prints in the edition.

When shopping for this kind of art, just remember that the value comes from the limited number in the edition. So, less is more...usually 350 or less is a good rule for value. Also, you will want to request documentation from the publisher stating that the piece is what the retailer says it is. Keep the original in your file and the copy with the art for insurance purposes. Whether the piece is numbered 1 or 101 does not affect the value.

Remember the publishing companies that are listed on page 73? Several of those companies also offer giclees, serigraphs, original, and commission pieces. The artists working with them are interested in offering their work in a variety of ways to the consumer. So if you love one particular artist, it is possible that the limited-edition fine-art pieces are also available through the publisher; and if the artist is prolific, he or she may be available to paint a piece on commission or at least have a selection of originals available.

I am often asked about the artist who has numerous pieces out in open editions and seem to be "everywhere." It makes me wonder if I won't see the same image on a plate in my favorite culinary catalog soon. Should I invest in those images? If the artist has many open edition reproductions in the marketplace, there are usually limited edition pieces available as well. If you can, purchase a limited edition. If you can't afford a good original, purchase a limited edition piece hand embellished by the artist or an open edition print of the best work. At least you know that in order to achieve that status, the artist must be one of the best!

Instant popularity may play itself out over time. We have all seen fads come and go. As with any fad in the marketplace, art works and artists can come in with a bang and fizzle out in short order with a sputter. There is no prescription to discerning longevity. However, fads can evolve into trends. I recommend making a purchase early on if you love the art. Don't go overboard. Watch the trend, and if it's still around after 2-3 years, buy more. It's like the fashion color lime green. When it returned from the 1970's after many years dormancy, the staying power was in question. It has remained steady in popularity for over 10 years!

In addition, the artist could eventually tire of producing reproductions and stick exclusively to doing commission and original work. Once an artist has gained international recognition, their originals sell for substantial figures and it may no longer be economically necessary to continue with reproductions. Exposure creates desire and demand. One of my clients purchased a painting from a street vendor at Ghirardelli Square in San Francisco in the 1970's. Leroy Neiman has since become highly acclaimed and his work is very valuable. So, the moral to the story is, "If you love it, buy it!" Who knows, your art may eventually or suddenly become rare and valuable.

PHOTOGRAPHY

I find in my work that there are some individuals who gravitate to the literal interpretation of art subjects that can only be achieved with a camera. Photography has truly become an art form. Many artists, especially those whose works appeared early in the 20th century, are highly collectible. And in recent years, with the advent of digital technology, we are privileged to experience the work of many contemporary artists who specialize in photography. Black and white photography is stunning in sophisticated and very simple interior spaces. If you are looking for a picture of a special place, you should explore local photography. Color photography has never been as realistic or as magnificent as it is today.

Photographic prints can be made from photographic negatives, positive transparencies or digital images, and printed on a wide variety of papers, including photo paper, fine art paper and canvas. The reproductions are often painstakingly made one at a time by the photographer.

The process used to make a silver print of a black and white negative differs from the process used to produce a color inkjet print from a digital file, but both processes must be under the total control of the artist from start to finish for optimum results. No other person, and certainly no machine, knows how the photographer wants the finished image to look. Only the photographer can make a finished print that exactly matches his vision. It can also be modified digitally by the artist, adding color and other effects and sold in limited editions, as discussed earlier. These works can very often be ordered from the artist in custom sizes.

Photography is also available in open edition by art publishing companies. Following the evolution of this art medium is fascinating!

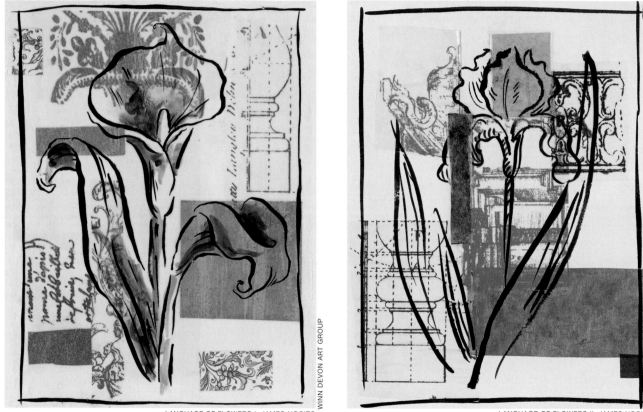

LANGUAGE OF FLOWERS I, JAMES NOCITO

LANGUAGE OF FLOWERS II, JAMES NOCITO

SERIGRAPH

Serigraphy, a process also known as silkscreen, was for many years the only means of fine art reproduction. You probably know silk screening as the method used to print T-shirts, but art serigraph printing is much more intricate! The artwork is created from a stenciled design worked into a nylon or wire mesh. The design is created by blocking out those areas that are not to be printed with a greasy substance applied to the screen, or with paper or other material. Once the design is in place, the mesh is positioned over high-quality paper and ink is pushed through it with a squeegee. Areas that are not blocked are printed. A different set of screens--and an additional pass through the press--is required for each color the artist wishes to print. In some cases 75 colors or more are required, layering the color to produce an image that best resembles the original piece.

When the artist, either alone or working with a master printer, creates the screens and prints the edition, each print is considered a "multiple original." The printing is complex and tedious. The coloring process is so intricate that it can take up to three or four months to complete an edition of average size. The real craft comes from a serigrapher's painting skills, eye for perspective, and artistic intuitiveness, something a computer can never have.

Serigraphy, like any other technology, has evolved in recent years. Now, most art is photographed and a transparency made. Then Mylar screens used for printing are made representing as many colors as needed. Computers are of growing importance in serigraphy, especially in making the screens. The printing process may also be done by machine instead of the "hand pulled" method. We are seeing more serigraphs printed on canvas, as well as fine art rag paper, always signed, numbered and limited in number of prints in an edition, creating value.

SERIGRAPH ON PAPER
EDITION SIZE: 275
IMAGE SIZE: 9 X 12

GICLÉE

A reproduction approach that is gaining quickly in popularity in the limited edition market is the giclee, pronounced "gee-clay." It starts with an image that is created or scanned into a computer, then printed on a high-speed, high-quality, inkjet printer. The term literally means "spurt" or "spray." Special inks produce incredibly true colors without the dot pattern associated with offset lithography, used by most printers for open-edition art reproduction. The best printers exude no less than one million droplets per second.

With advances in technology, the giclée has continued to evolve and has become an accepted fine art reproduction printing method. The quality of the inks used to print, and the substrate, or paper/canvas on which the image is printed, affect the quality and longevity of the print. A giclée can be either original art (when the image is created originally in the computer) or a reproduction (when an image is scanned into a computer, then printed.)

Because giclee is digital technology that is somewhat easy to apply, more artists have the opportunity to reproduce their images. It is the finest representation of the original available at this time. The art is digitally scanned. Because the printing process is also digital, the entire edition can be printed to order, or on demand, depending on the publishing company. Some companies offer custom image sizes on order. The pieces are limited in the edition and, of course, signed and numbered. They can be printed on canvas or fine art rag paper. If you see a fine-art, limited-edition piece that you want, do not hesitate to make the purchase. The giclee on the opposite page is very limited in number, only 50 in the world!

CERESTE, KENT LOVELACE
WINN DEVON ART GROUP
GICLEE ON CANVAS, EDITION SIZE: 50
IMAGE SIZE: 44 X 32

CUSTOM SIZE GICLÉE

Digital technology has changed the way the world now does business. By blending compelling imagery and applying the latest technology and commerce in an honest and high quality manner, a new standard for the art publishing industry has been created.

This approach allows for an image to be printed as a fine art reproduction, as it is ordered and to the size needed. Most custom giclee publishers offer the option of printing on paper or canvas. The giclee may be part of a limited edition, usually in an edition size of 375 and offered in multiple sizes including custom sizes. Each print is considered part of the edition to maintain the integrity of the print run. Price is appropriate depending on the size of the piece, substrate, and number in the run. The image selection is only limited to the digression of the publishers and imagination and talent of individual artists!

BORZOI ON THE SOFA, BERNARD DECLAVIERE

GRAND IMAGE

LOREN 4, MAEVE HARRIS

ABSTRACT FLORA I, MARY CALKINS

GRAND IMAGE

POISE, MATT LIVELY

BIG RED POPPIES, ELIZABETH HORNING

FINE ART "UNIQUES"

If you want something truly original and unique, then you must have an original. The term "unique" means original, one-of-a-kind pieces, or unique works. We are so impressed when we hear the term original in reference to art. Be assured that not all originals have value. Just because it's original doesn't mean that it is great art, right? So be careful when you are investing. The door-to-door peddler who sells original "copies" of Van Gogh is not a bargain!

Reputable galleries show and offer for sale pieces from those artists who have established credibility in the field. They have produced a body of work that is not only respected but desired in the marketplace. If you are doing serious shopping for original art, spend time in the well known galleries. Before taking your next trip, check out the gallery sites on line. You don't have to buy to enjoy and learn about good art. It's a process.

Do you have a favorite artist? It's fun to follow artists and see how they evolve and explore their creative bent. If you happen to find someone whose work is unknown and decide to collect, it can be especially rewarding to follow their career path. You may later boast about your discovery!

LAURIE BANNON, DESIGNER

THE POETS, CAROL JESSEN

THE DAYS OF WINE AND ROSES,
GILLES ARCHAMBULT

CORAL PASSAGES I, ELLIOT PARKER

MUSICAL, NIKOLAI RIMSKY

POLKA DOT POPPIES, HEATHER DONOVAN

TRANSLUCENCE II, DAVID BAILEY

SHADOWED MEADOW, SUNLIT PINES,
JON FRIEDMAN

TOBY, RON BURNS

VIN ROUGE, JAY ZIH JIAN LI

THE CANNON RACE II, CORY SILKEN

YOUNG GIRL READING, 1776,
JEAN-HONORE FRAGONARD

NEWTON'S GARDEN, TULIP III,
KEVIN PAULSEN

So, when it comes to choosing the "right" image, the choice is influenced by your taste, your style, your space, your colors, and your budget. Begin your search and document your finds. If the images work together, that is if the colors are compatible and they relate to your interior space and your style, and you love it... You will have the right image!

ART IMAGE WISH LIST

Publisher	Style #	Image Title	Artist	Size	Room
				X	
				X	
				X	
				X	
				X	
				X	
				X	
				X	
				X	
				X	
				X	
				X	

It's all in the design!

3

GREAT ART FRAMING DESIGN

Why is it that one framed image looks stunning and another just "ho hum"...? It could be the image itself, but then again it might be the *framing design*. When you purchase a framed art piece and place it in your interior space, sometimes it just doesn't work. Why is that?

There are three schools of thought concerning art framing design. The first is from the artist's perspective. An artist is concerned only about the presentation of the art, and rightly so. It is important that the art take "front and center" priority in relation to the design. No argument there! In most cases the artist would choose a white or off white mat and a non-descript frame moulding to complete the job. The artist's goal is to show the image, not the framing design.

©LOMA SMITH PHOTOGRAPHY

The interior designer looks at framing design in a slightly different way. The focus is to frame the image to enhance the space. Why not put a colored mat on the piece even though there is no color in the image? Hmmmmm…This could be called for in some cases, true. I have been known to do just that when the art does not repeat any colors in the room, but I believe that it is definitely not good design to compromise the image just to match the framing design to the space.

The picture framers must also weigh in! They usually have the opinion that the art should be framed solely to repeat the elements in the art. This is a good approach; however, there often are several great options for a framing design that will enhance the art. So, how do we know which approach to take?

Who is correct: the artist, the interior designer, or the framer? May I express my candid views based on experience in the interior business? Here goes…The artist, bless his heart, has selected the most reasonably priced framing solution to show his piece. If he does not have a gallery showing his work, he probably manufactured the frame and mat design himself. The purpose of the frame is to show the image in the least costly way. The real value is the art, not the framing. While the existing frame is functional, the new owner will likely change the framing before placing the art in their home or office.

The picture framer is really at a disadvantage because he sees only the image. It is rare that a picture framer will come to your home or office to evaluate your space. So, you or your interior or art designer can help by giving him the information that he is lacking. It is important to frame the art piece to enhance the image, but it is also important to take into consideration the space where it is going to be hung. I have learned over the years not to question another designer's framing design. The design elements in the space may have justifiable influence in the choice of framing design. Ultimately the goal is to choose the very best design for the art <u>and</u> the space!

ELEMENTS OF ART FRAMING DESIGN

Frame Moulding is the most visible part of the framing design. It is the single element that has the greatest impact on the design, but it also has the greatest impact on the price! Not all frame mouldings are equal. As with anything else we buy, there are Jaguars and VW's and everything in between. In our discussion I hope to give you an appreciation for the various manufacturers available in your framing stores and the differences in quality and styles.

Just like other products on the market, frame mouldings vary in price because of differences in quality. Materials and workmanship contribute to the value. For example, the stock used for the base will give you a clue to the price. If the wood is soft, the quality may be compromised. Remember the frame holds the art piece together. It is only as dependable as the wood from which it is made.

Country of origin also is a factor in the pricing of material. If it comes from Europe, there are shipping costs that must be factored into the price. Some of the most beautiful frame mouldings come from Italy. ROMA Moulding, a premier company, takes pride in the culture that has provided them with a strong appreciation of beauty and the ability to see its many facets. From the past to the present, whether in Rome or the rustic villages of Tuscany, they continue to be inspired by the remarkable architecture and the beauty of the land. It is the combination of an eye for design and their culture that enables ROMA to create the beautiful and uniquely designed collection we enjoy.

Another moulding manufacturer, Larson-Juhl, one of the oldest and largest frame moulding companies in the world, has international respect and prominence in the art framing industry. Finish is a considerable factor in the quality of frame moulding. Both Larson-Juhl and ROMA take pride in the hand painting, leafing, and distressing that go into their products. They use the finest quality of woods and combine various finishing methods to achieve the desired look. There are many ways that manufacturers create the finished look, from photographically assimilating a wood grain to the real thing. Some wood frames are real burl and others just look like it. That may suit your needs just fine, but it is important to know the difference so you know what you are buying. Solid wood is usually of greater value, just as in furniture manufacturing. Be sure to take a close look at the frame sample, noting "how" the finish look was achieved. Think of your art frame as the furniture on your walls!

Price can also be affected if genuine gold or silver leafing is used instead of foil. There are only a few companies who still offer the very time-honored art of making water-gilded frames. Why should American consumers who may see gilded frames only in museums not have access to these treasures for their own home? Craig Ponzio, CEO of Larson-Juhl, feels so strongly about quality that when he found the 100-year old Senelar atelier (studio) in Lille, France, he decided to acquire it! This highly skilled, hands-on process is centuries old and is used for applying gold leaf to a variety of surfaces. When gilding wood, one must layer the surface with a clay compound called bole and coats of paste like gesso to allow for the adhesion of the gold leaf. The tradition dates to the Phoenicians and Egyptians, who displayed elaborate gilding on many objects to convey regal status.

The amazingly thin, 10,000 leaves in a one-and-one-half-inch stack, are placed one at a time onto the gesso'ed frame and brushed with water to aid in adhesion. Once adhered to the surface, it is carefully rubbed with a sheep's-wool cloth, and then burnished to achieve the brilliant luster characteristic of hand water-gilding. Larson-Juhl offers these unique frames in two collections featuring replicas of the Louis XV and Florentine Renaissance periods. In addition, the Musee line takes a modernist approach with simple, clean lines. Ask for the water-gilding frames when you visit your framer next.

Lastly, the frame design contributes significantly to the desirability of the moulding and its demand in the marketplace, adding to value. While frames are often viewed as objects that merely hold art, they have been compelling works of art in their own right. The frame moulding manufacturer is constantly seeking to discover new and unique approaches to the frame profile or design. Whether the rabbet is high, placing the art away from the wall, or low, featuring a scoop to the frame, the styles are endless. With the many finishes and technological capabilities for duplicating carved and specialty woods available today, we are seeing choices that literally take your breath away.

TOP 8

WALL DESIGN DIVA'S
TOP 8 FRAME MANUFACTURERS

Price Category	Company	Comments
RIGHT UP THERE! Not every style in these lines is spendy. However, when you want something extra special they offer amazing frame mouldings.	Larson-Juhl	Quality, Timeless Design and Permanence
	ROMA Moulding	Fabulous "Fashion Forward" Styles and Finishes
	Picture Woods	Gorgeous Wood Finishes
QUALITY and VALUE These companies are known for their simple good looks and consistency of value.	Nurre Caxton	Terrific Transitional
	Studio Moulding	Beautiful Simple Style
	Nielsen Bainbridge	Good Looking Metal Styles
GREAT STYLE When you are looking for the frame that does the job and looks good too…	Universal	Awesome looks for the price!
	OMEGA	

Matboard is a paper or rag board used over artwork to separate it from the glass. It is generally made up of three layers: the face paper, the core and the backing. Matboards come in a wide variety of thicknesses composed of layers or plys, colors, textures and compositions.

Remember, I wrote earlier about the fact that one of the purposes of framing is to preserve the art? If you have ever taken an old framed piece apart, you will see the "acid burn" marking so characteristic of paper products. We have all seen how light affects newspaper. It turns dark yellow in just a few weeks, especially when left uncovered. You don't want that to happen to your valuable art piece!

Although preservation products have been available for just ten years, acid-free matboards have just recently become the norm as more people understand the benefit. Even open-edition art prints should be protected as they can discolor from paper products.

If a piece has value of a more personal nature, it deserves the protection of "Conservation Framing." Most pieces we bring to a framer should be framed with conservation in mind. As a rule of thumb, if the item you are framing is an irreplaceable, one-of-a-kind photograph, document or piece of memorabilia, or if it is an original work of art or a limited edition, it should be framed using conservation techniques and materials. The additional cost for "Conservation Framing" is marginal — and certainly well worth it.

A professional picture framer has the skills and materials necessary to preserve and protect your art piece as closely as possible to its original condition. Acid- and lignin-free mat and mount boards contain no impurities which can damage the art they surround. In 1995, Nielsen Bainbridge introduced The Alphamat® Artcare™ System - the first and only mat and mount boards that actively protect artwork from the damaging effects of air pollution and acids generated by the artwork itself.

You can easily identify an acid-free mat by checking the color of the bevel. The core of the mat board is usually a bright white color. If it is acid free, it will stay bright forever. If it is a regular paper mat, the color can yellow in 3 – 6 months, depending on the exposure to light.

Matboards can be carved, cut or painted to add decorative elements to the frame design. Various colors and textures can be stacked, spliced and combined in numerous ways. Mat board usually has a whitish material in the center so that a white line (bevel) shows when it is cut. However, some mat boards also have black or colored cores, resulting in a colored bevel when they are cut. Cores may be the same color as the face paper or a contrasting color. Colored-core mat board expands the design possibilities.

Matboard also comes in an extensive selection of fancy specialty styles, including linen, silk, suede, embossed and printed effects to assimilate faux finishes. The industry is sensitive to the fashion trends in interior design and stays current with the latest trends and looks.

Foam-core board is one of the elements in the framing design that is not visible. It is lightweight, plastic-centered board that is used as a mounting board, as a backing board, and as a spacer in deep frames or shadow boxes. Prints are usually dry mounted to foam-core board using heat and an adhesive film insuring a smooth appearance to the image. Otherwise you will see a ripple effect of the art. All poster art and photographs are dry mounted. However, with this method, the print can never be removed from this surface. Foam-core board also is used in routine mounting of needlework and paper art. I recommend that you ask for acid-free foam-core board for the same reasons that we use acid-free mat board. In the days before this product was available, framers used corrugated cardboard. Talk about acid!

For a valuable fine art piece, your professional framer will suggest another application called **Museum Mount**. However, technology is always changing as the market demands. Nielsen Bainbridge has introduced a new product that allows art to be reversed to its pre-mounting condition. **Artcare**™ **Restore**™ is an archival, heat-activated foam board. With this product, you can safely reverse art to its exact, pre-mounting condition. The non-permeable adhesive meets all archival standards and can be completely removed from the art. Artcare Restore's breakthrough adhesive activates at low temperatures and short drying times, making it safe for most art. Ask your professional about this product when framing anything valuable.

Glass or glazing is another part of the framing design that can be overlooked in importance. For years the only glass available was regular glass which allowed every kind of light to permeate the art. As a result, we experienced damage to art. The sad reality is that once damage from UV light has occurred, it can never be reversed. Ultraviolet light rays are one of the most dangerous elements that your artwork can encounter. It will not only cause your colors to fade to a mere shadow of their former glory, but will cause the materials themselves to begin to break down right in the frame. Have you ever seen a faded gum wrapper lying in the sun, bleached to a mere fragment of its original color? Perhaps the paper had become brittle as well — ready to break apart at the touch of a finger. The damage you saw was caused by the sun…specifically, the sun's damaging UV or ultraviolet light rays.

Ultraviolet light rays are the same villains that your doctor warns you about. They cause breakdown whenever they come in contact with organic materials, burning noses, bleaching gum wrappers and ruining your son's first finger painting. The damaging effects of UV light on artwork are cumulative and irreversible.

Unfortunately, the sun is not the only source of harmful UV light rays. All light sources, whether natural or artificial, have some of their components in the ultraviolet range. The most drastic visual effect of exposure to UV light is the dramatic fading of colors — especially those colors that contain red.

In the late 1990's the industries associated with paper and fabric conservation needs were blessed with glass products that could protect valuable pieces from fading and damage due to UV light exposure. **Tru Vue®**, one of the leading companies in the art framing industry offers Conservation Series® glass, insuring you that at least 98% of these most damaging light rays are filtered out before ever coming into contact with your valuables.

There are four types of Tru Vue® glass available that have UV protection. Be sure to ask your professional art framer about the glazing options available. What good does it do to frame your art if it fades within a year?

Before Exposure to Light

LOVE AND ROMANCE, VINTAGE

EDITIONS LIMITED GALLERIES

Light Damage

Have you experienced the effects of light damage?
We call this "blue art!" Don't let it happen to your important pieces!

A NOTE ABOUT PHOTOGRAPHY

The very nature of your photographs will dictate how they must be framed. Some photos are printed on papers which do not take well to regular heat-activated mounting techniques. Others, especially antique photos, are very sensitive to alkaline-based framing materials and, therefore, must be mounted and matted using special non-buffered boards.

All photos should be framed so that the glass is not touching the image. If it does, temperature and humidity changes may cause it to stick. This can potentially ruin the image. This can be accomplished two ways. A plastic spacer can be placed between the image and the glass just under the lip of the frame. The other way is to mat with conservation quality mat board. This will ensure that the photo emulsion does not touch the glass. It is also advisable to dry mount any photo that is not of an antique nature.

Design Tip:
Valuable photographs should NEVER be on continuous display. The best way to preserve an image is to have a copy made and frame the copy while storing the original in a dark and dry place.

TIMELESS ART FRAMING DESIGN

UNIVERSAL FRAMING PRODUCTS

Custom picture framing has greatly improved over the last 40 years. We now focus on enhancing the image visually and preserving it too! The product selection in the industry is endless, allowing choices that make our heads spin. With all of these choices comes a price. Custom picture framing is no small investment, but the value is there if the design is good. Even the "you-frame-it" shops, while competitive, are not inexpensive. Given that, it is desirable to frame your precious piece of art right the first time, incorporating the best design possible!

Keep the design simple and timeless is my advice. When I first began offering custom framed art to my clients I was enthralled with the oodles of matboard choices available. The more the better! As I gained knowledge and experience I realized that even though custom framing is a fashion business, it is smart to stay current with design trends but avoid temporary fads. Keep the design simple, utilizing quality frame styles, and only the mats and fillets necessary to create depth and enhance the art. Avoid over-design of the piece with complicated mat designs that compete with or *become* the art!

This is not to say that the framing design should be boring. By incorporating frame moulding and a mat design that is appropriate and in good taste, you will have not only a beautiful image, but a distinctive piece of art. Try to think of the framing design as the stage for the art. Without it, we cannot appreciate the true talent shown in the image.

SIGNS OF BAD DESIGN

Improper proportion of mat to frame...

Proper proportion is vital in all good design. The width of the mat border should never be the same as the width of the frame. This draws the eye away from the art. The frame should always be smaller than the mat border. If you own an image you love and the framing design looks like this, you will be amazed how great it will look if you just update the framing design!

EXPLORER'S CLUB, POLLY THOMPSON

WILD APPLE GRAPHICS

THE LAST GREAT ROMANTIC, JACK VETTRIANO

THE ART GROUP

Skimpy mat width

Generous mat widths are now recommended for even very small images. My general rule is at least 4" of total mat width including multiple mats and fillets. Use wider mat borders to balance the scale of a large room or furnishings. The mat width at the bottom should be slightly wider than the sides and top to create a classic look and increase perceived value. Dramatic mat design can do wonders for perceived value!

Inappropriate mat color or style...

Wrong colored mats are the "death of an image." The border is the dominant element in the design and steals from the quality of the art. Blend the mat to the background to allow the most important elements in the image priority. Neutral mat colors allow the color in the image to stand out. Matching accents in the image with a strong mat color is not a good idea as you see here. However, repeating a color in a second mat can be very effective. Be careful to do this only if it truly enhances the image.

GARDEN BOUQUET, LIZ JARDINE

WINN DEVON ART GROUP

KITCHEN STILL LIFE II, LORRIE LANE

WILD APPLE GRAPHICS

Bad choice of frame moulding for image...

Choose frame styles that are in proportion to the weight and style of the art. Pay attention to the period and design elements in the imagery. Think about your space and the relationship of the art to the other elements in the room. Also, when framing set or pairs you may want to use a smaller frame than you would if the art is standing alone. Be careful when choosing color in the frame. Best not to try to match the colors in the image!

105

GOOD ART FRAMING DESIGN IS NOT "ROCKET SCIENCE!"

Balance, proportion and interest are basic principles of all good design and art framing is no exception! Our desire to achieve excellence in The Fine Art of Wall Design is one of the many reasons to custom frame.

FRAMING DESIGN WITH NEUTRAL COLOR MATS

This image is beautifully presented in a classic timeless style. It is set off with a "border" created by either a mat or self border closest to the image. Next to this border is a narrow line of a contrast color. A wide neutral mat completes the look by creating a wide enough border to give the image breathing room. The frame finishes the look by repeating the contrast color. This application is smart especially when the interior space is not defined and subject to change. Without question, the look is simple, classic, timeless and straightforward.

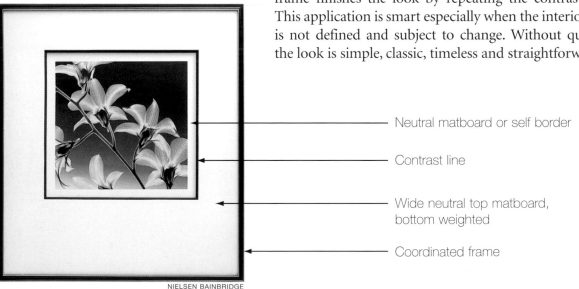

NIELSEN BAINBRIDGE

Neutral matboard or self border

Contrast line

Wide neutral top matboard, bottom weighted

Coordinated frame

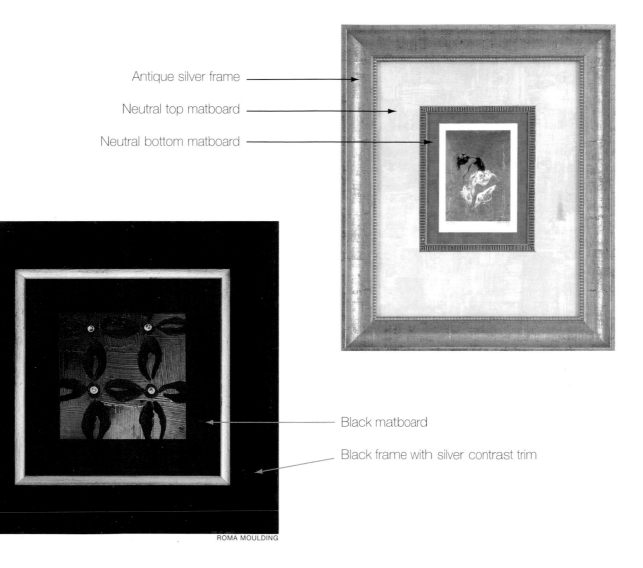

Antique silver frame

Neutral top matboard

Neutral bottom matboard

Black matboard

Black frame with silver contrast trim

ROMA MOULDING

107

ART FRAMING DESIGN
WITH DRAMATIC CONTRAST

There are interiors and images that call for a dramatic approach to design. The framed image shown on the left has a black background and the mat color is light creating contrast. The other piece features a simple image with a dark mat. In both cases the image "pops" because of the dramatic difference in weight and color. The bold contrast causes your eye to focus on the image. The interior spaces where these images will hang call for the added touch of drama and formality. One is traditional and the other transitional to modern.

Mat color tip: When designing for art I always look for elements in the image that warrant repeating. Please avoid multiple color matching in mat design, however. The mats should never overwhelm the image. Look away and then look back at the design. What do you see...the image or the mat? It is easy to get carried away with the fun choices we have for framing design! Remember that the image is the reason you are showcasing the piece.

The mat width shown in all of these pieces is equal on the sides and top, and weighted slightly on the bottom. I recommend at least 1/4" to 1" for most pieces, depending on the size. By "weighting" the mat at the bottom, the eye perceives a feeling of proportion and stability that is not necessarily obvious at first glance. This is a feature that is indicative of custom framing. You may not see this in most mass-produced framed art.

Contrast black matboard

Simple frame and fillet repeats gold in image

LARSON-JUHL MOULDING

Ornate frame & fillet repeats the lines in image

Black background in image

Contrast matboard

ROMA MOULDING

109

ART FRAMING DESIGN
WITH EXCITING MAT WIDTH EFFECTS

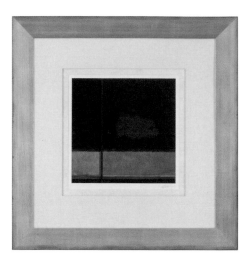

ROMA MOULDING

You can create a completely different look by varying the width of the mat. These framed pieces feature the identical art image. What a difference!

If you have a square image and need a finished piece that is taller than wide, you can weight the mat at the bottom. It will create interest and pizzazz in your living space!

Notice that the mat proportions are slightly different in each of these pieces. The images are the same and the outside frame dimensions are also the same, but the mat proportions are different.

Classic Bottom Weight

Asian Scroll Design

2-Left/2-Top/2-Right/4.5-5-Bottom

2-Left/3-Right/2-Right/5-6-Bottom

ROMA MOULDING

FILLET (FILL – IT!)
THE FRAME WITHIN A FRAME!

A fillet is a mini frame moulding. It is manufactured and finished just like the larger frame moulding. It is usually about 1/8" to 1/2" in width and is designed to be placed next to and under the opening edge of a mat. It can also sit next to and under the lip of the frame. Fillets are wonderful enhancements to art framing design. They are as varied in style as frame mouldings and match or contrast the frame itself. The possibilities are endless! I love fillets!

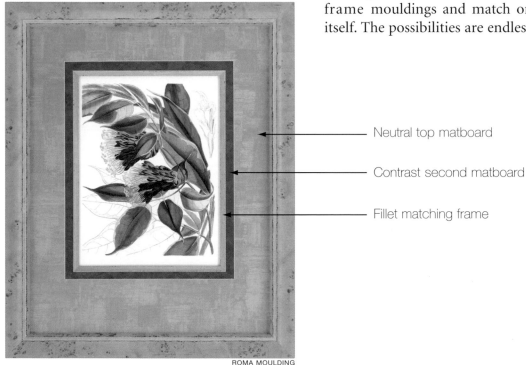

Neutral top matboard

Contrast second matboard

Fillet matching frame

ROMA MOULDING

112

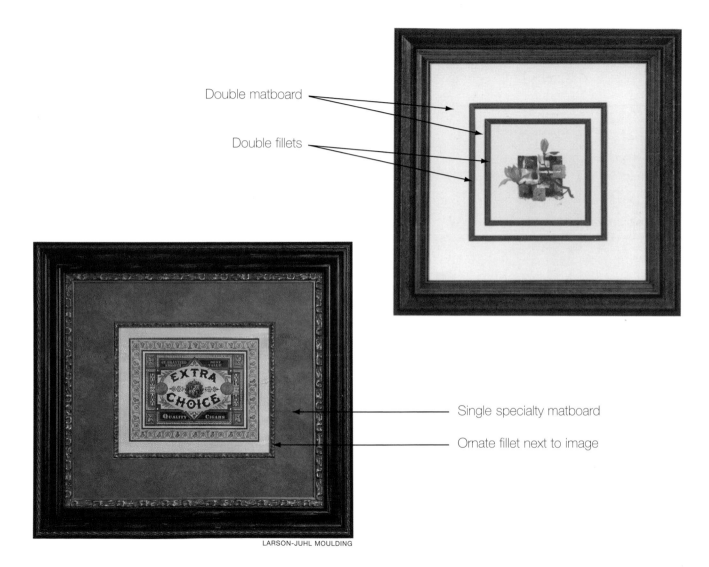

Double matboard

Double fillets

Single specialty matboard

Ornate fillet next to image

EXTRA
CHOICE

GUARANTEED
SMOOTH   BEST
VALUE

QUALITY   CIGARS

LARSON-JUHL MOULDING

FRAMING DESIGN FOR SMALL IMAGES

Small images can be the most creative pieces you will ever own! It is such fun to design a small image. There is room to incorporate multiple mats, fillets, and varying matboard widths. When framed with creativity and flair they become amazing pieces of art!

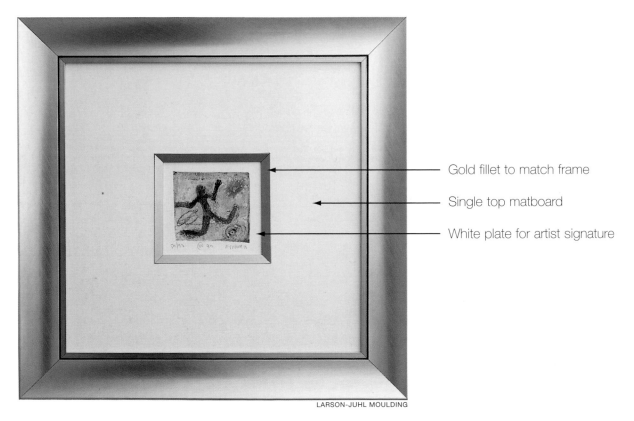

Gold fillet to match frame

Single top matboard

White plate for artist signature

LARSON-JUHL MOULDING

114

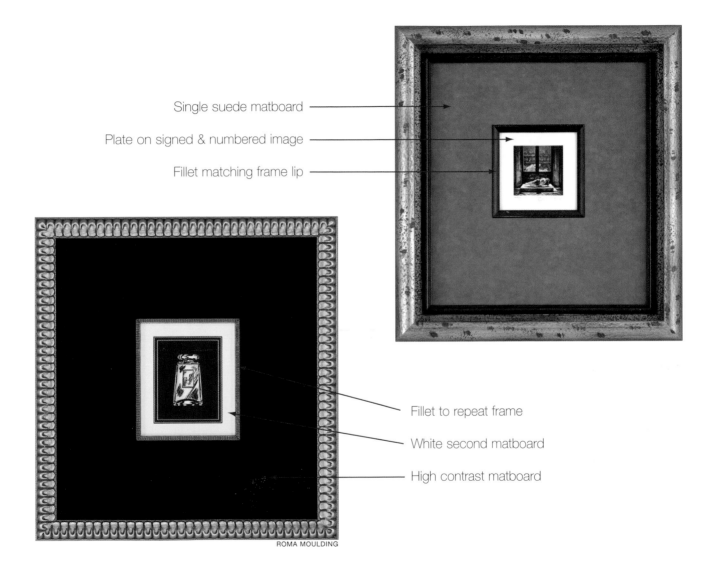

Single suede matboard

Plate on signed & numbered image

Fillet matching frame lip

Fillet to repeat frame

White second matboard

High contrast matboard

ROMA MOULDING

115

FLOAT YOUR IMAGE...NOT YOUR BOAT!

Float in framing terms is a means of securing artwork to a rigid support so all edges are visible. The technique may be used when the image extends to the edge of the paper, or the edges are "deckled" or torn. The mat upon which the art is floated can be any color of course and the image also looks wonderful if lifted off the mat with a foam core platform behind it. Then a second mat, with a fillet or bevel accent can be added to further enhance the image, wow! All of these design techniques add to the presentation creating interest and depth!

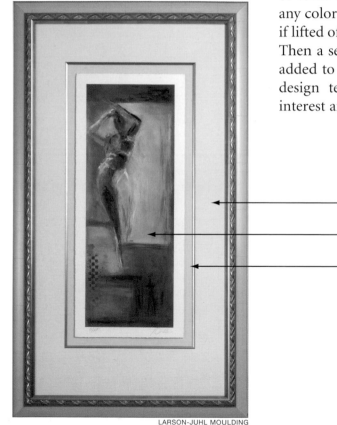

Top matboard with fillet

Floated image

Bottom matboard behind image

LARSON-JUHL MOULDING

116

BEVEL ACCENTS

Bainbridge Artcare has developed Beveled Accents. It is beveled foam board that is wrapped with archival papers and fabrics. It is placed under the opening edge of a mat opening, creating rich depth and dimension to your art. It is a terrific way to enhance your image. The look is transitional and is very cost effective.

NIELSEN BAINBRIDGE

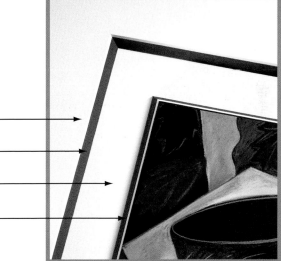

Top white mat

Teal bevel accent

Bottom mat, behind image

Floated image, mounted on teal matboard
cut with reverse bevel

117

CREATE A "PIECE OF ART" FROM SOMETHING YOU TREASURE

Did I tell you earlier that most custom framing designers are especially talented when it comes to creating art from the simplest objects, objects you love and want to preserve. They may remind you of a day gone by or a special event. Art framing is the best way to showcase your treasures and create a unique piece of art!

SINGLE OBJECTS

When designing object art, treat it like one dimensional art for design application. The colors shown here enhance the pieces and create a classic look. The mat colors are subtle, giving the art "front and center" importance.

LARSON-JUHL MOULDING

118

What fun, bragging about the amazing hole-in-one! How do they do that? The tee is beautifully situated in the niche provided by the mat design and the ball carefully placed in its place of honor. The green suede mats couldn't say it any better. Last but not least is the image of the hole where it took place!

LARSON-JUHL MOULDING

You sold the turntable but the memories of that place in time lives on. What a creative way to frame the record jacket and the disc with the label that tells the story!

COLLECTIONS

What to do with all those unusual forms of currency from your world travels? Frame them and you have a wonderful conversation piece and a great piece of art!

Then there is the key collection from your great uncle's barn. This piece is a representation of history and a lovely geometric art piece!

ROMA MOULDING

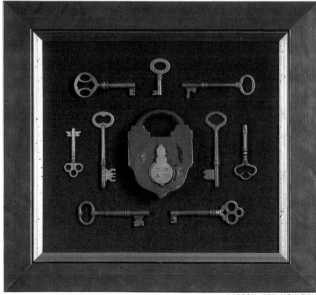

LARSON-JUHL MOULDING

FRAMING FAMILY PHOTOGRAPHS

Framing photographs is so satisfying. It is the documentation of our heritage, the preservation of a place in time only you can relate to. Photographs can be formal or casual. The most important thing to keep in mind is keep it simple. All of the wonderful framing elements are appropriate for these images.

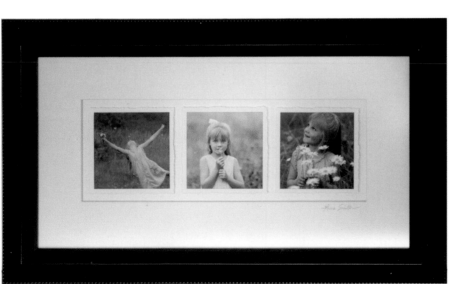

LOMA SMITH PHOTOGRAPHY

Family "walls" are wonderful. They can be as attractive and decorative as your most spectacular framed art images. Some of the most famous subjects in paintings were members of "royal" families of ages past. Treat your precious memories as art!

LARSON JUHL MOULDING

FRAMING TO THE IMAGE

Canvas and laminate art pieces are designed without glass and matboard. They can be simple or elaborate depending on the image.

ROMA MOULDING

SMALL IMAGE-WIDE FRAME

This example features a wonderful design utilizing a wide moulding for a small piece.

FRAME FINISH AND COLOR MAKES THE DIFFERENCE

Look how much color and style of frame moulding can change the look of an image. Which frame do you like best on these images? They are all beautiful! It comes down to the space where they will be displayed.

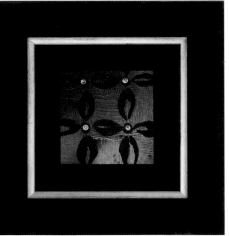

ROMA MOULDING

THE MORE FRAMES THE BETTER!

By layering or stacking two or more frames in tandem with fillets you can create interest and a look that is one-of-a-kind, just for you! There is more than one frame on each of these pieces.

LARSON-JUHL MOULDING

TWO FRAMES, ONE FILLET   TWO FRAMES, ONE FILLET

THERE ARE NO "RULES" WHEN IT COMES TO CHOOSING A FRAME, BUT GUIDELINES ARE GOOD...

ROMA MOULDING

Color and style are very important. Look for elements in the image that are repeated in the frame, both in color and style. This is a classic look that will always work in every space.

Even if you are not a designer it is valuable to develop a discerning eye for good design. The more examples you see the better! Are you getting the picture?

LARSON-JUHL MOULDING

SURPRISE!
SURPRISE!

Don't be afraid to do something completely out of the ordinary. It creates interest and an element of...surprise! Abstract art can be wonderful framed with traditional ornate moulding.

LARSON-JUHL MOULDING

WALL DESIGN DIVA'S
ART DESIGN TIPS

- Begin with an image you love. Custom frame it.

- Don't just frame your art, preserve it!

- Use conservation matboard and foam core to avoid acid burn.

- UV protective glass is sunscreen for your art!

- The frame is the most cost variable part of the framing investment. Look for quality *and* value.

- Incorporate fabulous frames, fillets, and matboard to enhance both the art and your interior space!

- Develop a discerning eye for good design.

- Now you have a "piece of art, not just a picture!"

Everything in its place! 4

THE RIGHT PLACE
OR NO PLACE!

You have found the art you love and want to place in your interior space. You have selected the framing that best enhances the image and the space. But wait! What about how and where to hang it? This is a "Chicken-Egg" dilemma. What comes first: Image Selection, Framing Design, or Placement?

All of these decisions are interrelated and need to be addressed in tandem. It is helpful to understand all of the elements of The Fine Art of Wall Design before proceeding with the process of image selection, framing design, and placement. One does influence the other. The Fine Art of Wall Design is achieved through an understanding of all the design elements presented here.

©LOMA SMITH PHOTOGRAPHY

For example, as we have discussed in the proceeding chapters, the decisions about framing design hinge on the desired finished size of the piece. If you know where it is going to be hung, then your framing decision may be influenced by placement. If you have many options for placement, then there will be no restrictions on size. However, if the art has limitations regarding framing design then placement may be driven by the piece size.

In my experience, placement is critical and arguably the most important element in achieving the Fine Art of Wall Design. It can make or break an interior space. If the art placement is right and dynamic, the rest of the décor will follow suit. If the décor is wonderful and the art placement is wrong, the interior look will be compromised. Not only that; but the beauty of the art is compromised!

There is always price consideration in relation to every design decision. Money spent on fabulous art will be for naught if the pieces are not well placed. Conversely, if you understand placement, you can pull off a terrific look for a reasonable investment.

So, get ready to discover the basic design principles of placement that will transform your interior and help you create the Fine Art of Wall Design. You too, will be able to say, *"Va Va Voom", "Ooh La La", "WOW!"* *"Ah Hah"* and *"That's it!"*

HIGH OR LOW, NOW YOU KNOW
WHERE IT SHOULD GO!

• Hang art for viewing from either a sitting or standing position, whichever is done most in the space.
• Relate the art to its surroundings.
• Hang art about 4" to 9" or a hand width above a sofa, chair railing, or table.

In this example the art is hung too high. It does not relate to the sofa. Do you get the impression that there is a helium balloon carrying it skyward?

LARSON-JUHL MOULDING

133

Notice the relation of the art to the fireplace mantel. It is about 8" above the mantle. Do not divide the available space top to bottom and then center the art. It is acceptable for the space above the art to be greater than that below. The pieces to the right and left are just clearing the chair backs so that they are eye level for those viewing them from a seated position. Don't be afraid to mix styles. It works!

Place art on a table or shelf as long as the proportion is good. The look is casual and works beautifully if appropriate. In the event of an earthquake or other catastrophe, secure the wire on a hook for security. Angle the piece about 1-1/2" to 2" from the wall.

Art can be placed very high if it is anchored by another art piece in a grouping or a piece of furniture. Lovely!

TOO BIG, TOO SMALL - YOU CAN KNOW IT ALL!

• Cover at least 2/3's or 3/5's of the space to provide scale with the furniture.

That means that if your sofa is 5' wide you will need to cover at least 3' of space with art or other wall décor. The art piece pictured here is less than half the width of the sofa. It doesn't quite have the weight needed for balance. We have the feeling that something is missing; skimpy in proportion.

LARSON-JUHL MOULDING

The proportion shown here is pleasing to the eye. The image is wide enough to accommodate the chairs and table arrangement. Ceiling height and overall spaciousness of the room carries the height of the piece.

Placement Tip:
Larger pieces require more room for the viewer to stand back and enjoy — hang these pieces opposite the entrance to a room, at the end of a corridor, or in a spacious room with high ceilings.

© RUSS WIDSTRAND

LAURIE BANNON, DESIGNER

SUZANNE GALLAGHER, WALL DESIGN DIVA

©RUSS WIDSTRAND

WEIGHT & BALANCE... IT APPLIES TO ART, TOO!

FORMAL - SYMMETRICAL BALANCE

Symmetrical balance is achieved when there is perfect symmetry between objects in a grouping. If you can draw a line down the middle you will see exactly the same thing on both sides of the line creating equal balance. This approach seems to lend itself to a more formal look. It is the easiest to achieve well. People who have "A" type personalities are often more comfortable with formal balance. The rooms shown on pages 41, 44, 62 and 134 are good examples of formal balance.

INFORMAL - ASYMMETRICAL BALANCE

Asymmetrical balance is achieved when weight is evenly distributed throughout a grouping, but the elements may be different sizes and shapes. If you draw a line down the center the two halves will not be alike. It is more difficult to achieve good asymmetrical balance. Sanguine personality types tend to like this type of balance. I love to see both forms of balance in every room for variety and interest!

Art becomes part of the furniture arrangement. The art shown here is placed to the left of center in order to create space for the table lamp. The arrangement is simple. The height is good also, just slightly higher than the lamp as the art is the focal point. It relates nicely to the table.

KIMBERLEE JAYNES INTERIOR DESIGNS, INC.

140

• *In general...the greatest weight should be on the BOTTOM and to the LEFT in any design arrangement.*

Take a look at this grouping. Do you feel slightly uneasy? That is because the weight is to the RIGHT and to the TOP. The large floral still life image is the heaviest piece, to the right. The heaviest of the pair to the left is placed at the top. There is no cohesiveness of the pieces except for one element, color.

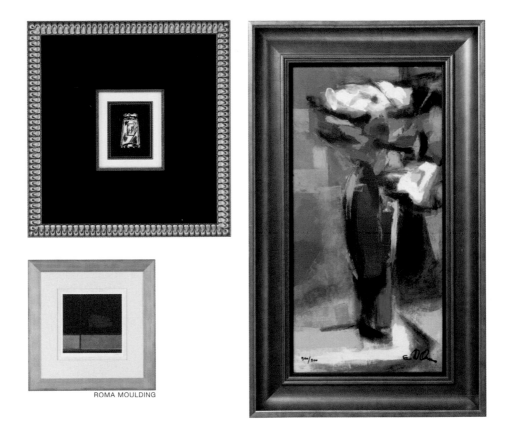

ROMA MOULDING

The arrangement here is much better. The largest piece is to the left and the weight is at the bottom. Looking good! Color is the one element that pulls this grouping together. In every grouping you should be able to draw an invisible straight line from side to side and top to bottom. The eye likes to rest on these quadrants.

LARSON-JUHL MOULDING

Place art so that it draws you from room to room along with the wall color and the rest of the furnishings.

Create variety and interest by mixing styles of art and furnishings. Art is the soul of the room, giving it personality and pizzaz!

SUZANNE GALLAGHER, WALL DESIGN DIVA

©RUSS WIDSTRAND

TIPS FOR HANGING ART, NOT YOURSELF!

Tool Kit: Pencil, tape measure, hammer and picture hangers are essential. Spackle comes in handy to fill in those rare mistakes. A tool that is a "gotta have" is a ruled level. These are inexpensive and enable you to measure and get it straight the first time!

Wire Hanger: Hold the art against the wall to determine where you want to place it. Make a small pencil mark on the wall at the top center. Take the art down. Pull the wire taut as if the art was hanging. Measure the distance from the top of the frame to the highest point of the taut wire. Using your ruled level, measure down that same distance from the mark the on the wall to determine the center of the placement for hooks. If you are centering your piece, double check your mark in relation to the furniture and adjust. Place the center of the ruled level on the pencil mark and measure 5 to 12 inches on each side and mark location of hooks. The distance between hooks depends on the size of the piece. A 40" piece will need hooks at least 24" apart, and so on. This keeps the piece from tipping side to side easily. Pound hooks into the wall and hang art.

Your art piece may be large and too heavy to hold. No problem. Measure the height of the art piece. Pull the wire taut and note that measurement. Then take your tape extended to the height of the piece and place it against the wall where you want the center and top edge of the art. Adjust the tape until you have the desired height. Make your pencil mark, not at the top of the tape but the same measurement down from the top of the art piece to the wire. Proceed to mark position of hook placement using the ruled level, place hooks and hang art.

Saw Tooth Hooks: Hold the piece of art where you want to hang it with the image toward the wall. Make a light pencil mark on the wall at the top edge of the frame above the center of each hook. Take the art down and check markings with a ruled level. You will need to measure down about ?" to adjust for the placement of the hooks, re-mark. Erase the original pencil marks. Pound nails or brass nail hooks at marked locations. Traditional hangers will not work with the saw tooth hook. Hang art.

FRAMED ART GROUPINGS

I am often called in to place art and mirrors for a client who has made a big move to a smaller home! One of the _most_ satisfying projects for me is to arrange art that a homeowner has collected over the years. The first step is to identify the focal points of every room giving priority to the most important living spaces. I group pieces together that may have never been together before, reframe some that are out of date, and add a few new images to spice things up. The feel of their spaces can be completely changed with new art arrangements incorporating the images that are loved most!

When hanging art together in a grouping the end result can be creative and really great or really wrong. The trick is to recognize when the latter is true and why. It is smart to follow some simple design principles to achieve the best results.

Unless you are striving for an eclectic "antique shop" look, the pieces in the groupings should look as though they belong together. Select frame and matting styles that are compatible to create a balanced, unified look to the group as a whole.

There are five general categories of groupings that I will share with you. Think of each as a guideline and an inspiration for your unique style!

- **Pairs/Trios**
- **Diagonal - Stairs**
- **Rectangular**
- **Oval**
- **Triangular**

PAIRS - TRIOS

Hanging pairs and trios, usually two or more similar images framed alike is an easy concept to grasp. When hanging a pair side by side it is best to keep them close enough together so that they feel connected. A good rule of thumb is 1.5" for small pieces up to 4" for larger ones. If placed too far apart the pieces look like they are negative charges repelling one another.

ROMA MOULDING

146

Pairs can be hung in multiples of two or more side by side or one above the other. Pairs are also wonderful placed on either side of an architectural piece such as a window or fireplace. Formal balance!

These two pieces are perfect side by side. The spacing is right, just enough to breathe and relate to one another. The space above the sofa is good.

ROMA MOULDING

STACKED PAIRS

I loved designing this framed pair of canvas transferred open edition prints for my client. Colette has a variety of styles incorporated in her home and these two abstract images anchor the landing on her stairway. They are seen from her entry and the energy of color pulls your eye up the stairway. Beautiful!

TOP: WINGED VICTORY, NOAH LI-LEGER
BOTTOM: APOLLO, NOAH LI-LEGER
CANADIAN ART PRINTS

©RUSS WIDSTRAND

SUZANNE GALLAGHER, WALL DESIGN DIVA

This is a simple straightforward approach to placing art; classic and very appealing. A group of images that are framed identically are called a "set." A grouping that is different in imagery and framing design is referred to as a "collection." The spacing for a set is best when the pieces are placed the same distance apart on all sides. Although it is easy to design, it is one of the most difficult to hang! Perfection and patience rule.

ROMA MOULDING

149

TRIOS

Trio Groupings can be placed one above another or side by side. The rule of three is especially good in an informal setting. They can all be the same size or different sizes. Keep the visual weight at the bottom. This grouping is well spaced on the wall in relation to the furniture and the ceiling.

KIMBERLEE JAYNES INTERIOR DESIGNS, INC.

Remember the exterior doors in the 50's that had small windows staggered diagonally across the upper portion? It may have been chic at the time but promise me you will not follow that example when hanging art. It is only appropriate when you are placing art on a staircase.

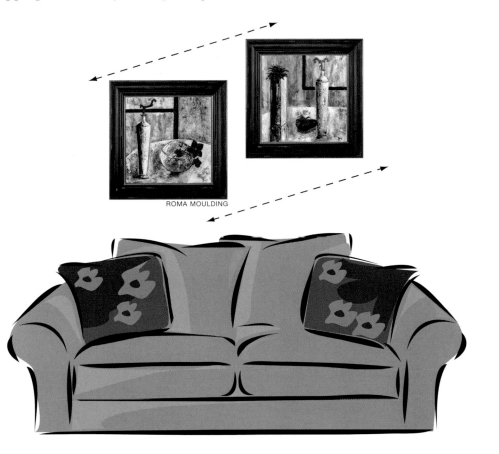

ROMA MOULDING

151

What goes up must come down, except for a staircase. Bring the eye back to earth with a complimentary descending line!

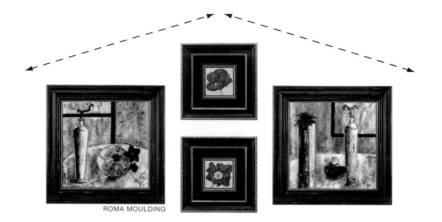

ROMA MOULDING

This is the one place where art looks fabulous when placed diagonally. If you want your eye to travel upward, then a diagonal arrangement will work.

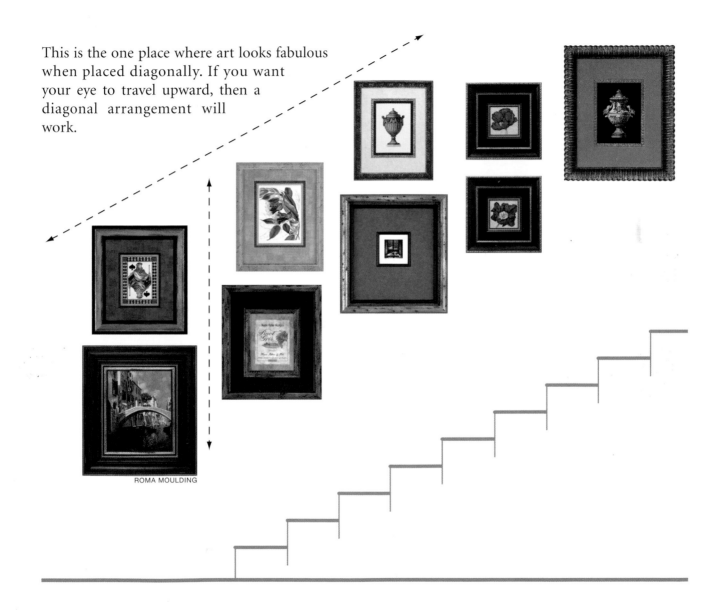

ROMA MOULDING

Stairs…the options are endless! Don't be afraid to mix styles. Just be sure the elements relate to one another.

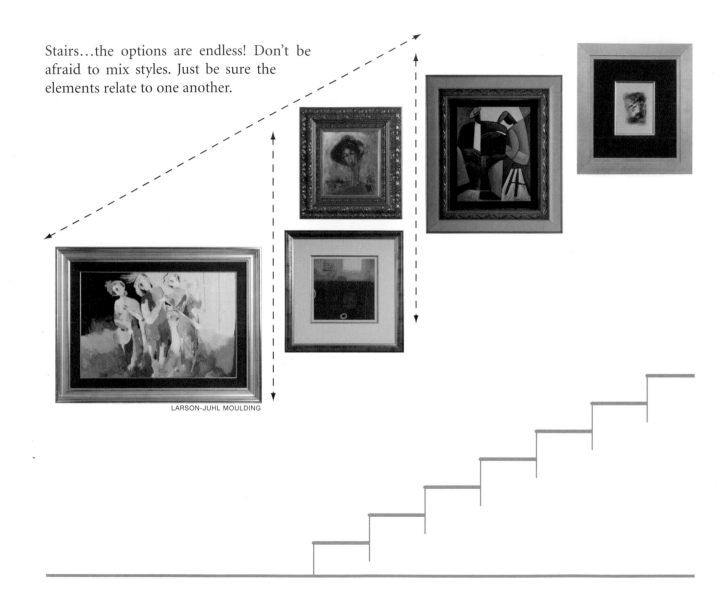

LARSON-JUHL MOULDING

What a lovely staircase! The niche in the corner becomes part of the art grouping going up the staircase. The art continues the line up the staircase, a perfect application of a diagonal grouping.

LAURIE BANNON, DESIGNER

©RUSS WIDSTRAND

Small stairways are just as deserving of art display as grand ones. This piece fits beautifully in the space and can be viewed when moving up the stairway as well as from the entry hall and the living room. It lends color, interest and personality to the space.

Placement Tip:
Hang small, more detailed pieces in small spaces such as hallways and corridors, between doorways where the art can be enjoyed up close and personal.

SUZANNE GALLAGHER, WALL DESIGN DIVA

Groupings are the most creative and unique way to display art in any space. It is such fun to pull pieces together and achieve The Fine Art of Wall Design with items that individually made little impact.

The easiest way to tackle the project is to lay the plan out in a graphic shape...

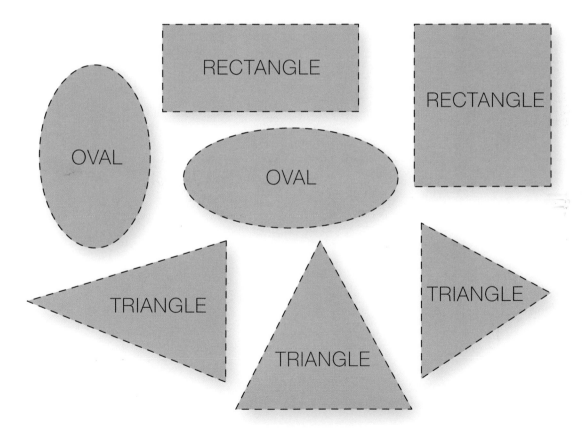

This is one of the easiest shapes to work with. Here we have the major piece in the center. The two maps are heavier in visual weight than the sailing ship photograph, so we placed them on the left.

SUZANNE GALLAGHER, WALL DESIGN DIVA, LAURIE BANNON, DESIGNER

©RUSS WIDSTRAND

The weight is at the bottom of this delightful grouping of Van Gogh pieces. Based on the 2/3's rule, perhaps the piece over the head of the bed could be joined by another, don't you think?

M FRANCES INTERIORS

©RUSS WIDSTRAND

TRIANGULAR SHAPED GROUPING

Triangular groupings can be placed with the anchoring side perpendicular to the floor as shown here. The stairway ascends upward creating a perfect opportunity for this triangle to be turned on it's side. This would also be an appropriate application on either side of a mirror, as pictured on page 168. Triangular groupings work well with the anchoring side parallel to the floor to create interest over a piece of furniture or to bring attention to a high ceiling. See page 152 for an example of this.

THESE ANTIQUE FANS ARE COLLECTORS' ITEMS AND HAVE A PROMINENT PLACE IN THE ENTRY OF THIS HOME. THEY ARE FRAMED INDIVIDUALLY FOR PRACTICAL REASONS IN ADDITION TO DESIGN APPEAL. IF THE OWNERS DECIDE TO MOVE TO ANOTHER HOME THEIR ART WILL ADAPT TO ANOTHER LOCATION MORE EASILY IF IT CAN BE SEPARATED.

©RUSS WIDSTRAND

SUZANNE GALLAGHER, WALL DESIGN DIVA

TIPS FOR HANGING ART GROUPINGS

Option I. Visualize and Go! Lay art out on floor to determine the best arrangement. Measure outside dimensions to make sure arrangement fits area. Starting with the largest piece or center piece, hang. Continue with each piece to the right and left.

Option II. Gotta Love Graph Paper! Measure each piece of framed art and create a template to scale of your graph paper. Design grouping arranged on graph paper. Using the plan determine where to place the center piece, hang. Continue with each piece to the right and left.

Option III. Big as Life! Place art on construction paper and trace around to make a template that is the same size as each piece to be hung. Cut out paper templates and write description of art on each template. Mark location of hanging nails or hooks on the templates. Using masking tape, arrange paper templates on the wall. When you are satisfied, mark location of hanger with a push pin through the paper into the wall. Remove paper template one by one, locate mark for hook. Hang art. Proceed with each art piece.

Tip:
My favorite hooks are the brass Floreat hangers. They cradle the fine steel nail at the proper angle and leave only a tiny pinhole when removed.

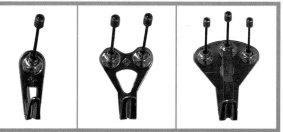

ZIABICKI IMPORT CO.

MIRROR, MIRROR ON THE WALL…

Mirrors should always reflect something beautiful. They can also be placed effectively where space is limited and needs to appear larger. This mirror reflects the beautiful art piece hung over the fireplace mantle in the living room. It expands the space in the front hall, and by reflecting the art piece brings added color into the space.

SUZANNE GALLAGHER, WALL DESIGN DIVA

©RUSS WIDSTRAND

SUZANNE GALLAGHER, WALL DESIGN DIVA

Mirrors can be used to simply create interest. They are wonderful in groupings with art and other wall décor. By incorporating a variety of interesting and unique frame mouldings you will enhance the arrangement significantly. Frames are works of art in themselves!

M FRANCES INTERIORS

LIGHT UP YOUR LIFE BY LIGHTING YOUR ART!

Although lighting can be a challenge for many homeowners, don't be intimidated. There are two basic lighting techniques: ambient "room" lighting or "spot" lighting. Ambient lighting sets a mood in the space and is usually indirect. It provides casual light, allowing the work of art to blend in with the rest of the room.

"Spot" lights, bring attention and make a piece "pop" — a nice touch for really special pieces. "Spot" lighting is dramatic. There are many ways to direct light now with the advent of can lighting and light strips that affix to the wall or the ceiling. Often builders will place a can light with an "eyeball" attachment directing the light toward the wall over a prominent space such as the fireplace or entry wall. Light fixtures designed to attach to the art are also available. They have small inconspicuous shades and light bulbs; bringing attention not to the fixture but to the art where it should be.

WALL DESIGN DIVA'S
ART LIGHTING TIPS

- Unless you have used a reflection control glass on your art, choose subdued lighting effects that will not reflect directly into the glass of your art piece.

- Bring attention to special framed pieces with individual picture lights.
  Use lower wattage bulbs to avoid creating shadows on a deep frame.
  If possible hide the wiring. You may want to place the art over a furniture piece so that wiring can be concealed. Some light fixtures have battery power.

- Avoid hanging your valuable artwork in direct sunlight. Even with protective UV-blocking glass, prolonged exposure to the sun's heat can destroy the art.
  I recommend protecting all of your furnishing in the home by professional application of a window tinting product. This will protect your furnishings against 99% of harmful UV light.

- Use incandescent light bulbs which feature only 4% of damaging UV light rays. Fluorescent lights, on the other hand, have a high concentration of UV rays. This is another reason to protect your art with UV protective glass, especially in commercial spaces where fluorescent lights are abundant.

SENSE OF BELONGING, DONNA YOUNG, GRAND IMAGE

WALL DESIGN DIVA'S
WALL PLACEMENT TIPS

- Hang art for viewing from either a sitting or standing position, whichever is done most in the space.

- Place framed art 4" – 9" or a hand width above a sofa, chair railing or table.

- Cover 2/3's or 3/5's of the space to provide scale with the furniture.

- Create balance, formal or informal in an arrangement.

- In general the greatest weight should be on the bottom and to the left in any design arrangement.

- Arrange art in a grouping close enough so that pieces relates to one another.

- Create at least one vertical and one horizontal line to give the eye a point of reference.

- Diagonal placement is for stairs, thank you!

- Arrange art groupings in geometric shapes. i.e.: rectangular, oval, and triangular.

- Place mirrors so they reflect something beautiful.

GROVE ON THE WATER'S EDGE, GREG STOCKS

POEMS ART, INC.

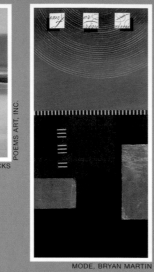

MODE, BRYAN MARTIN

HADDAD'S FINE ARTS

TROPICAL BREEZE, JOHN CANNING

WINN DEVON ART GROUP

POLKA DOT TULIPS, HEATHER DONOVAN

TRUE STORY, VINTAGE

EDITIONS LIMITED GALLERIES

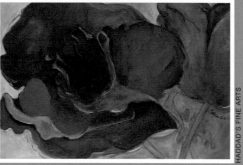

POPPIES IN THE SUN, GHISLAINE

HADDAD'S FINE ARTS

GUIDEPOST, VALERIE WILLSON

WINN DEVON ART GROUP

CALLA LEAF II,
STEVEN N. MEYERS

POEMS ART, INC.

EXOTIC ELEMENTS I, SANDY CLARK

HADDAD'S FINE ARTS

BOOM BOOM ROOM, LARRY GROSSMAN

EDITIONS LIMITED GALLERIES

BLUE CAR, DANNY O

WILD APPLE GRAPHICS

PASO ROBLES I, JANINE CLARKE

TOP ART

YES, YOU GOT THE PICTURE!

Have you enjoyed learning about The Fine Art of Wall Design? My hope is that you have a new understanding about art and its relationship to interior design. Will it be the inspiration for your next project? Furnishing your home is an exciting journey of self discovery. It is the one place where you can be surrounded with all the things you love. It is *your* personal haven. Now, give it your personality and pizzaz with art!

172

Appendix

ART TERMS AND DEFINITIONS

Acid burn – A brown line or brown coloration on paper that is the result of prolonged contact with acidic cardboard or other materials. Acid burns often are seen on the face of paper artwork that was matted with acidic cardboard mats.

Acid-free – A term used to describe adhesives, papers, matboards and other framing supplies that have no acid in them. Acid-free materials should be used when framing works of art on paper. Matboards, mounting boards, tapes, envelopes and other framing materials all are available in acid-free varieties. Some have been chemically treated to remove impurities; others, such as those made of 100 percent pure cotton rag, never contained acid and are generally the best choice for framing fine art.

Acrylic – Clear plastic sheeting used in framing applications. Acrylic can be used instead of glass to glaze a picture; acrylic also is used to make boxes to hold large pieces and three-dimensional objects.

Alpha – Term used by Bainbridge Matboard Company to connote acid-free matboard. See Rag.

Animation art – Artwork produced from animated films; may be described as "cels" referring to celluloid on which such films were produced. Some prints on paper also may be produced from animated cels.

Artist's proof – (This may be penciled in at the bottom of a print as A/P) Prints outside the standard edition which are intended for the artist's own private collection and use as part of the original artist-publisher agreement.

Backing board – General term for the material used to fill the back of the frame; most often scrap matboard or foam-core board. The backing board is held in place by glazier's points or brads and is covered with a dust cover (Kraft paper, usually). The English refer to mounting board as "backing board." So, too, do some U.S. conservators.

Bevel – Generally refers to the 45-degree angle on the window opening of a matboard that has been cut with a mat cutter. When such a cut is made, the core of the matboard is exposed. A standard bevel, which leaves the core of the matboard showing around the window opening in front, is cut from the back of the matboard. Unless otherwise specified, it is this cut that framers generally mean when they refer to the bevel.

If a mat is cut with a reverse bevel, the 45-degree angle cut slants away from the surface of the matboard so the matboard core is not seen from the front. A reverse bevel often is used when a visible bevel would be a distracting element in the design.

Black Core – Mat that has a core which is black.

Bloom – A white or milky haze on an oil painting. It is caused by water vapor in the painting varnish.

Border or Plate – A decorative, colored, or white edge surrounding the image.

Canceling – To prevent further use of a printing plate after an edition has been printed, the artist sometimes "cancels" the plate by X-ing it out or in some other way defacing it. Sometimes cancellation proofs are made. However, many artists who make woodblock or other relief prints save individual blocks and combine them in different designs.

Cartoon art – Original drawings/paintings of cartoonists that were originally produced for newspaper comics or editorial cartoon pages.

Cast paper – Artwork produced by placing wet paper or paper mache materials in a mold and allowing it to dry. The result generally looks like a plaster cast of an image, but is very lightweight.

Chop mark – An un-inked, embossed stamp on a print which identifies the printer, artists, workshop or sometimes a collector. Also called a "blind-stamp."

Compo – Short for "composition," which is a plaster like substance used in making decorative ornaments for frame finishing. Compo ornaments are applied to a wood frame base to give moulding an ornate, hand-carved look. Compo also can be used to repair or replace ornaments on a frame.

Conservation framing – Using materials and techniques in the framing process to ensure artwork is not damaged by framing. Hinging the artwork instead of mounting it, using high-quality acid-free boards and mats, using non-staining paste, and glazing with conservation glass or acrylic are generally accepted procedures used to help preserve artwork. The same procedures are sometimes referred to as "preservation framing."

Conservation mounting – The process of attaching the artwork to the backing board in a way that will not harm the art. Materials used include rag board, rice or wheat paste, and mulberry hinges, or other inert (non-deteriorating or non-staining) materials and processes. Many framers call this process "museum mounting" or "preservation mounting."

Colored Core – Mat that has a colored core.

Crafts – Any of a number of items produced using original art techniques are today considered fine art crafts--blown glass, pottery, ceramics, clay pieces, textiles/weavings, wood carvings and other items that are created by artists are original and unique works of art. Some are very expensive and are very collectible.

Crop – Reducing of the image size. Oversized prints are often cropped to eliminate the necessity for oversize mats. A slight amount of cropping will rarely affect the look of the framed piece and is an accepted industry practice.

Deckle Edge – A torn or uneven edge on a print that can often be a featured element in the framing design. Print publishers sometimes note "deckle edge" in their catalogs.

Distressing – A technique sometimes used on furniture and picture frame moulding to literally beat up the object with chains or other implements and leave random gouges in the wood before finishing. The treatment makes wood look old and worn.

Documentation – Information available on the edition of a print telling the artist's name, the printer's name, the location of the workshop, the number of prints in the edition, date, etc. Although this is somewhat important in print collecting, the condition of the print usually is more significant.

Dry mounting – prints are mounted to a surface using heat and an adhesive film insuring a smooth appearance to the image. With this method, the print can never be removed from this surface therefore; you must Museum Mount valuable fine art. Most all poster art and photographs are dry mounted.

Dry mount, dry mounting – The process of using dry adhesive tissues to mount paper artwork or photographs to a board, using high heat and a dry mount press.

Dust cover – A protective paper sheet (usually kraft paper) attached to the back of the frame to protect the contents from dirt. The dust cover often is attached with ATG tape laid along the frame edges; a variety of glues also may be used to attach the dust cover.

Edition – The total number of prints made of a specific image and issued together from a publisher.

Embossing – A raised three-dimensional surface on the artwork. Print publishers usually note embossing in their catalogs. If incorporated into the design, this feature will enhance the finished image.

Fabric Wrap – Mats are hand wrapped with fabric. Designer or framer may provide fabric. Alpha or rag mats are required, but foam core can also be wrapped for a deep bevel accent. Fabric is adhered to mat and wrapped around to the back side covering beveled edge. Beautiful effect!

Foam-core board – A lightweight, plastic-centered board sold in large sheets. Foam-core board is used as a mounting board, as a backing board, and as a spacer in deep frames or shadow boxes. Foam-core board also is used in routine mounting of needlework and paper art. Foam-core board variations come from many manufacturers, with different compositions, colors and face papers.

Fillet – (fill-it) (1) a very thin moulding used as an accent in framing inside another moulding or liner. It is sometimes used under the glazing at the edge of the mat window opening. Some framers also refer to edge of an undermat (a thin border that shows around the artwork) as a fillet.

(2) Any thick piece of paper or board or thin piece of wood glued to the moulding rabbet to hold the glass away from an un-matted piece of artwork. Another term for "fillet" in this second usage is "spacer."

(3) The decorative wood moulding placed behind a mat to create the effect of a "frame within a frame". A fillet may also be placed against the inside of the frame to add decorative dimension to the molding itself. Depending upon the size of your fillet choice, it will count as 2 or 3 components when determining your framing design.

Fitting – The process of putting together the pieces of the framing package: the joined moulding, glass, mounted artwork, matting, backing board, dust cover and hardware. Fitting includes cleaning the glass and checking the entire job for flaws before closing the frame.

Float (or Tipping) – A means of securing artwork to a rigid support so all edges are visible. Technique may be used when the image extends to the edge of the paper.

Foam Core Spacer – Piece of foam core placed under mat to create more depth in art design. It is recessed back from beveled edge of mat out of sight.

Foxing – Mold growth on paper artwork (typically appearing as brown spots). Foxing is found particularly on old prints and graphics, maps, letters and other documents.

French Line – A line drawn on a mat usually following the outline of the mat opening. May be any color.

Gesso – A brush-on white primer used as base coat over raw moulding prior to painting or leafing.

Gilding – The process of applying gold leaf and/or burnishing powders to a prepared wood frame. See "gold leaf."

Giclée – An image that is created or scanned into a computer, then printed on a high-speed ink-jet printer. (The term literally means "spurt" or "spray.") Special inks produce incredibly true colors without the dot pattern associated with offset lithography. With advances in technology, the giclée has continued to evolve, and has become an accepted fine art printing method. The quality of the inks used to print, and the substrate on which the image is printed, affect the quality and longevity of the print. A giclée can be either original art (when the image is created originally in the computer) or a reproduction (when an image is scanned into a computer, then printed.)

Glazing – A broad term that includes a wide variety of glass and acrylic products used to finish and protect framed artwork. Varieties include regular picture framing glass, conservation/preservation glass and acrylic, anti-reflective and non-glare glass. Many manufacturers carry products that offer combinations of these features.

Graphic – A term for any "multiple original" work of art on paper. The graphics media includes intaglios, serigraphs, and lithographs. An offset reproduction is not a graphic.

Gold leaf – Very thin leaves of real gold that are burnished onto a wood frame that has been coated with several layers of other material in preparation. The process is painstaking and expensive because of the use of precious metal.

Hinges – Materials used to mount artwork in conservation framing. Strips of Japanese or mulberry paper are torn; starch glue is applied to the strips. The paper art is attached to the acid-free mount only by these hinges. In recent years, a number of hinging products have been introduced, including strips of paste-impregnated mulberry paper that are water-activated.

Intaglio – From an Italian word meaning "cut in," intaglio prints are made from images cut below the surface of the printing plate. Ink is forced into these cut-out images and then forced onto the paper in a press exerting great pressure. Intaglio prints include etchings, aquatints, drypoints, engravings, soft-ground etchings and mezzotints. In some processes, the lines are cut out by hand with tools; in others, they are bitten out by acid.

Joining – The process of putting together mitered sticks of moulding to make the frame. Joining requires applying glue to each corner, carefully placing the segments in the vise or joining machine, and then attaching the corners. If placed in a vise, the corners can be nailed by hand. If placed in a power joiner such as an underpinner, the segments will be held together by staples or wedges inserted by the machine from underneath. The nails are important because they hold the corner together firmly until the glue dries. However, glue is most important to provide a strong joint that will not separate easily.

Lacing – The conservation-approved way to mount a variety of types of needle art prior to framing. The artwork is centered on a mounting board, and the excess fabric is wrapped to the back of the board. With a needle and thread, the framer draws cotton thread through a corner of the fabric on one side and across to the opposite side; he continues back and forth across the work as if lacing a shoe.

With lacing completed across two sides, the work is turned and the pattern is repeated for the remaining two sides, until the work is held firmly in place around the support board. Lacing is time-consuming and painstaking work.

Laminate – The process in which 100% of the art is adhered on a dense board. The finished product is reflection free. Brush strokes or texture can be added. No mats or glass are used in this application.

Laminate (moulding) – Moulding featuring high-gloss plastic, leather, wood or other material applied over a wood core.

Leafing – The process of applying real gold or silver leaf or imitation leaf to a moulding or mat.

Limited edition – This term refers to the number of objects that are available. In art, a limited edition refers to the fact that the article is one of a number of images in a published edition for which a predetermined number of impressions were from a plate. Once the pre-determined number of impressions is made, no more impressions are to be taken; assuring that the edition is "limited." The number of impressions in a limited edition should be information that is available to the consumer. Both original graphics and reproductions are offered as "limited editions" from artists and art publishers.

Limited edition reproduction – (Sometimes referred to as "offset lithograph.") Art that has been photo mechanically reproduced from another medium and printed by one of several methods, often by offset presses. The edition size has been predetermined by the publisher, generally based on the artist's popularity and sales potential.

Original graphics also are "limited editions," but prints produced by original means--and do not exist already in another medium--are considered multiple original prints, not reproductions.

Lip – The thin, projecting edge of the moulding that is just above the rabbet; mats and glazing generally fit under the moulding lip.

Liner – A moulding, usually fabric-covered, used inside the outer moulding in a frame design. A liner is not completely finished, so it would not be used as the only moulding for a frame. Liners often are used in place of mats on framed oil paintings.

Lithography – Artwork printed from a stone or metal plate or other flat surface. The artist uses a greasy substance to draw on the surface of the plate; only these greasy areas will accept ink. Once the plate is inked, high-quality paper is laid over it and the package is pulled through a press. To create a lithograph with a number of different colors, a number of different plates must be prepared and the paper must go through the press each time a new color is added. Lithographs are usually printed in editions of several hundred. Each print is considered a "multiple original" because the artist pulled each one from the press, or closely supervised the press operator. Each print is signed and numbered in the margin.

Matboard – A paper or rag board used over artwork to separate it from the glass. Matboard generally is made up of three layers: the face paper, the core and the backing. Matboards come in a wide variety of thicknesses (plys), colors, textures and compositions, and many acid-free matboards are for conservation framing.

Matboards can be carved, cut or painted to add decorative elements to the frame design. Various colors and textures can be stacked, spliced and combined in numerous ways.

Matboard usually has a whitish material in the center so that a white line (bevel) shows when it is cut. However, some matboards also have black or colored cores, resulting in a colored bevel when they are cut. Cores may be the same color as the face paper or a contrasting color. Colored-core matboard expands the design possibilities for framers.

Matting – The process of cutting and placing a piece of matboard, with a window opening cut, over or around artwork. The mat serves two functions: It protects the artwork by separating it from the glazing and providing air circulation; and it enhances the artwork it surrounds. It may be a highly decorative part of the design, or it may simply provide a restful area around the artwork.

Mitering – The process of cutting two corresponding angles in sticks or lengths of moulding. When joined together, the angles form the corner of the frame. A square or rectangular frame uses 45-degree miter cuts; frames with triangles or other shapes in the design require other angles for the miter.

Mixed media – Artists often combine two or more printmaking methods to produce unique mixed-media works. Sometimes collage techniques are added to prints to produce a mixed-media piece.

Monotype – The only type of print that comes in an edition of one. The artist draws or paints on a flat surface, then lays fine paper over the surface and pulls the package through a press. Because no fixed design has been created in the plate, the design can never be exactly duplicated. However, artists can partially re-ink the plate and run it through a press in successive printings, creating a series of prints similar to the original. These are known as "ghost prints."

Monotypes are signed and numbered in the margin 1/1 indicating one print from an edition of one.

Moulding – The material used to build a frame. Mouldings can be wood, metal, plastic or laminate, and they may be purchased from suppliers in lengths/sticks or as chops.

Mounting – The procedure of securing artwork or an object to a surface to hold it in the frame. There are many methods of mounting, including dry mounting, wet mounting, spray mounting, and vacuum mounting, lacing, stretching, stapling and hinging. It is important to choose the proper method to preserve the value of the items being mounted.

Museum Mounting – Conservation framing of fine art with 100% acid free materials. Acid free mats are available. A special mounting with acid free tape or hinges allows the print to hang freely. Fine art is never Dry Mounted. Depending upon the weight of the paper, there may be a slight wrinkling effect during temperature and humidity changes. This is normal and indicative of fine art.

Non-Glare Plexi – Plexi Glass that is also treated to be Non-glare.

Non-Glare Glass – Glass etched with acid to minimize glare. Available, however not recommended as image appears distorted. It usually blocks only 53% of UV light.

Non-glare glass – A glazing, usually etched on one or both sides, which eliminates reflections and glare from room lights.

Offset lithograph – A photo mechanically reproduced image. See "limited edition reproduction."

Open edition reproductions – Photo mechanically reproduced images that are published with no restrictions as to the number of copies that will be made. Open editions usually are decorative pieces of art done in current colors, subjects and sizes, printed on inexpensive paper.

Painted Bevel – Bevel of mat is painted. May be any color. Can be used to hide yellow core of paper mat, or just to enhance design.

Pair or Grouping – If pieces are to hang as a pair or grouping, you must specify on a Special Instruction Sheet to guarantee dye lot match on mats and frames.

Paper Size – the dimension of the entire print including any writing, captions, border, etc. as stated in the print publisher's catalog.

Photography – Photographic prints can be made from photographic negatives, positive transparencies or digital images, and printed on a wide variety of substrates, including photo paper, fine art paper and canvas. They can be black and white or color. Many artists, especially those whose works appeared early in the 20th century, are highly collectible. A number of contemporary artists also specialize in photography.

Plexi Glass – Glazing made of acrylic. An option on any piece. Acrylic glass will not shatter when broken like regular glass.

Plastic Spacer – Narrow clear plastic rod placed under Frame Lip after glass is inserted to separate the art from glass. This is especially important when framing photos and there is no mat. Otherwise in time the photo will adhere to the glass and be damaged.

Poster – This art medium comes from the ancient practice of "posting" messages in public places. Used for advertising or other communication needs, posters were designed to communicate quickly and graphically. Posters are still used for that purpose today--movies, concerts, plays and other public events all are promoted with posters.

However, posters also are produced strictly as decorative art, usually inexpensively on inexpensive paper. Posters almost always photomechanical reproductions; there is always graphic type on a poster, which is the primary difference between these and open edition reproductions.

Vintage posters – those printed 50 to 100 years ago – are highly collectable and have investment value. These often are very large and very graphic, with subject matter ranging from entertainment events to advertisements for products such as tobacco, wine and household items. Many early poster artists have become very famous.

Prints, printmaking – "Print" is a generic term for a single graphic made by a variety of printing techniques. Once the term was applied only to original graphics, but in recent years, produced by offset presses and other printing methods also have been referred to as prints. The techniques used to make prints often are referred to as the "printmaking processes."

Profile – The shape or design of the moulding, including all carved or grooved elements.

Rabbet – The groove under the lip of the moulding that allows space for the mat, glass, art and mounting board. The depth of the rabbet determines the number of components that can be put in a particular frame.

Rag board – A board manufactured from cotton or other fibers that are acid free acid free. Virgin rag board was the only choice of conservators for many years and is still considered a high-quality choice for conservation framing. However, many conservators today find that chemically neutralized colored boards made of purified wood fibers also are acceptable for use in conservation.

Used for conservation framing and mounting always or for art that may be subject to fading. It is now the preferred choice for all framing because it does not fade and will protect all art for the long term.

Restoration – Work done on a piece of artwork to make it resemble its original condition. It really isn't "restoring," since nothing can bring the art back to its exact original state. Restoration may involve relining, in-painting, cleaning, re-varnishing, etc., and is generally best left to experts in the field.

Restrikes – Modern-day printings of antique prints. Restrikes can be made from the old plates used to make authentic prints, or they can be made from new plates created just for the restrikes. These prints should be labeled as a restrike, to differentiate them from original antique prints.

Reveal – The desired dimension of each mat showing beneath the top mat. The standard width is usually 1/4", however you may show as much or as little, 1/8" as you wish.

Reverse Bevel – Mat openings are cut with a standard bevel edge showing the core of the matboard. This is standard; however the edge can be back cut so that the core does not show.

Regular Glass – Standard clear glass is included in the framing price.

Security Locks – Special locking mechanism used typically in commercial application to secure art to the wall.

Sculpture – Images created in three-dimensional form in a wide variety of materials--clay, bronze and marble are most common. Some sculpture pieces are reproduced from molds and are considered to be "published" works. Others are unique pieces created entirely by the sculptor.

Serigraph – (Also known as a silkscreen.) Artwork created from a stenciled design worked into a nylon or wire mesh. The design is created by blocking out areas that are not to be printed with a greasy substance applied to the screen, or with paper or other material. Once the design is in place, the mesh is positioned over high-quality paper and ink is pushed through it with a squeegee; areas that are not blocked are printed. A different set of screens--and an additional pass through the press--is required for each color the artist wishes to print.

When the artist, either alone or working with a master printer, creates the screens and prints the edition, generally several hundred of an image, each print is considered a "multiple original." Some reproductions also are now produced using serigraphic techniques, and are called serigraphs.

Signed and numbered – At the bottom of each print in an edition, the artist pencils in his signature and numbers the print. The numbering appears as one number over another, for example, 15/30. This indicates that this was the 15th print to be signed and that there were 30 prints in all.

Spandrel frame – A frame made with a circular or oval opening within a square or rectangle.

Specialty Mats – Mats with specialty finishes such as metallic, marble, silky.

States (first state, second state, etc.) – While an artist is pulling proofs of a print, he may make changes or corrections which alter the plate. Each time a plate is changed, it is said to be in a "state."

Stretcher – A support frame made of wood onto which the canvas of oil paintings or needle art can be mounted. A stretcher has adjustable corners that allow for periodic tightening (stretching) of the canvas, unlike a strainer (see above) which is solidly joined at the corners.

Stretch – Canvas art is stretched on wooden bars, and then placed in frame. Needle art is laced. It is laced across the back, not stapled to the wood frame, as is canvas art. Our framer can provide this service.

UV Glazing – Treatment for glass or Plexi to protect contents from 97% of ultraviolet light. Protects art from fading and sun damage. It should be used on anything of historic, investment or sentimental value, such as original art, limited edition prints, heirloom photographs and needle art.

Unique – In art, this term is applied to original artwork. All original, one-of-a-kind pieces are unique works.

V-Groove – The process of cutting two close, facing bevels into matboard so they form a "V" when the board is taped back together. It allows core to show through

Vacuum mounting – A cold mounting system using the pressure of a vacuum press to mount paper art and fabrics to a mounting board. Either sprays or wet adhesives such as paste can be used.

Vacuum press – A press that creates a vacuum to generate enough pressure to mount artwork to a backing board. Some presses are combination heat/vacuum presses.

Wet Mounting – Method of mounting art on paper by using some type of aqueous adhesive to affix the paper to another surface. Art is mounted to a backing by use of a wet adhesive.

Weighted Mat – a design option created by specifying a wider Mat Margin on the bottom side of the image.

CONTRIBUTORS

ART IMAGERY

Allan Bruce Zee Fine Art Photography
Allan Bruce Zee
2240 SE 24th Avenue
Portland, OR 97214
503-234-3211di
abz@spiritone.com
www.allanbrucezee.com

Editions Ltd. & Drybrush Graphics
Michael Jakola, CEO
4090 Halleck Street
Emeryville, CA 94608
510-923-9770
mjakola@editionslimited.com
www.editionslimited.com

Encore Art Group
Canadian Art Prints &
Winn Devon Art Group
110-6311 Westminister Hwy.
Richmond, British Columbia
Canada V7C 4V4
800-663-1166
sales@encoreartgroup.com
www.canadianartprints.com
www.winndevon.com

Grand Image Ltd.
Lindy Gillespie, COO
3201 First Avenue South, Ste. #201
Seattle, WA 98134
206-624-0444
service@grandimage.com
www.grandimage.com

Haddad's Fine Arts, Inc.
3855 E. Mira Loma Avenue
Anaheim, CA 92806
714-996-2100
mail@haddadsfinearts.com
www.haddadsfinearts.com

Image Conscious
George Leeson
1261 Howard Street
San Francisco, CA 94103
800-532-2333
415-626-1555
gleeson@imageconscious.com
www.imageconscious.com

New York Graphic Society
Owen F. Hickey
129 Glover Avenue
Norwalk, CT 06896
1.800.677.6947
203.846.2105
www.nygs.com

Old World Prints
Lonnie Lemco
8080 Villa Park Drive
Richmond, VA 23228
804-213-0600
LLemco@OldWorldPrintsLtd.com
www.OldWorldPrintsLtd.com

Poems Art, Ltd.
Nasser Shotorbani &
Laurie Downing
PO Box9990
Salt Lake City, UT 84109-9990
801-747-1344
info@poemsart.com
www.poemsart.com

Russ Widstrand
WIDSTRAND PHOTOGRAPHY
www.widstrand.com/editions

The Art Group
Sara Richards
33 Cherry Hill Drive
Danvers, MA 01923
978-762-8612
srichards@artgroup.com
www.artgroup.com
www.insidespace.com

Top Art
6490 Mar Industry Place, Suite D
San Diego, CA 92121
858-554-0102
usainfo@topartweb.com
www.TopArtweb.com

Wild Apple Graphics
John and Laurie Chester
526 Woodstock Road
Woodstock, VT 05091
802-457-3003
sales@wildapple.com
www.wildapple.com

Will Rafuse
Artist
www.willrafuse.com

FRAMED ART IMAGERY

Larson-Juhl
3900 Steve Reynolds Blvd.
Atlanta, GA 30093
800-886-6126
www.larsonjuhl.com

Nielsen Bainbridge
40 Eisenhower Drive
Paramus, NJ 07653
800-342-0124
info@nbframing.com
www.nbframing.com

ROMA Moulding
Tony Gareri
360 Hanlan Road
Woodbridge, Ontario
Canada L4L 3P6
800-263-2322
tgareri@romamoulding.com
www.RomaMoulding.com

Universal Framing Products
21139 Centre Pointe Pkwy
Santa Clarita
CA 91350US
P: 661.362.6262
F: 661.362.6263
sales@universalframing.com
www.universalframing.com

ADDITIONAL IMAGERY

Ziabicki Import Co., Inc
Floreat Hangers
Diana and Charles Gretzinger
PO Box 081004
Racine, Wisconsin 53408
262-633-7918
www.ziabicki.com
info@ziabicki.com

INTERIORS

DP Design
Diane Plesset
ASID, CMKBD
PO Box 480
Clackamas, OR 97015
503-761-7294
diane@dp-design.com
www.dp-design.com

Green With Envy Interiors
Evelyn and Dian Green
503-531-8665
designer@greenwithenvyinteriors.net
www.GreenWithEnvyInteriors.net

Kimberlee Jaynes Interior Designs, Inc.
NWSID Associate Member
503 407-9525
kim@kimberleejaynes.com
www.kimberleejaynes.com

KP Design Group, Inc.
Kathie Pozarich
4690 Auburn Lane
Lake Oswego, OR 97035
503-635-3400
KPDesignGroup@comcast.net

Laurie Bannon
ASID Allied Member
503-330-1579
LaurieBannon@comcast.net

M Frances Interiors
Mary Frances Naftzger
2690 Glen Eagles Road
Lake Oswego, OR 97034
503-675-0136
Mfrancesint@comcast.net

Renaissance Homes
16771 Boones Ferry Road
Lake Oswego, OR 97035
503-636-5600
www.Renaissance-Homes.com

Sue Raymond
ASID Allied Member
Parker Furniture Design Center
Beaverton, OR
psraymond@comcast.net

Suzanne Gallagher
Wall Design Diva
ASID, Industry Partner
NWSID, Professional
Resource Affiliate
503-579-ARTS (2787)
Suzanne@WallDesignDiva.com
www.WallDesignDiva.com

INTERIOR PHOTOGRAPHY

WIDSTRAND PHOTOGRAPHY
Russ Widstrand
Portland, OR
(503) 777-7085
russ@widstrand.com
Architecture:
  www.site-light.com
Fine Art:
  www.widstrand.com/editions

Bruce Forster Photography, Inc.
Bruce Forster
1325 NWFlanders
Portland,OR 97209
503-222-5222
studio@viewfindersnw.com
www.bruceforsterphotography.com

PORTRAIT PHOTOGRAPHY

Loma Smith Photography
Loma Smith
West Linn, Oregon
503-638-9997
Loma@LomaSmith.com
www.LomaSmith.com